TEACHER'S MANUAL

CONTEMPORARY ENGLISH
BOOK 2

Mechelle Perrott

Jan Forstrom

CONTEMPORARY BOOKS

a division of NTC/CONTEMPORARY PUBLISHING GROUP
Lincolnwood, Illinois USA

Cover Illustration: Regan Dunnick

ISBN: 0-8092-0708-7

Published by Contemporary Books,
a division of NTC/Contemporary Publishing Group, Inc.
© 1999 NTC/Contemporary Publishing Group, Inc.,
4255 West Touhy Avenue, Lincolnwood (Chicago), Illinois 60646-1975 U.S.A.

9 0 VL 9 8 7 6 5 4 3 2 1

Contents

Scope and Sequence: Literacy

Unit	Topic	Culture Focus	Literacy Skills	Functions	SCANS Competencies
Unit A	Preliteracy		Shape recognition, directionality, recognizing, tracing, copying uppercase letters		Foundation Skills
Unit B	Preliteracy		Shape recognition, directionality, recognizing, tracing, and copying lowercase letters; matching uppercase and lowercase letters; numbers 1–10		Foundation Skills
1	Human Relations: Greetings	Greetings at school and work	Interpreting and identifying ideographs signifying male and female; sight word recognition	Greetings; stating one's name	Foundation Skills
2	Numbers	Counting	Recognizing, tracing, and copying numbers; matching numbers and quantities; understanding numbers 1–20	Repeating words for clarification	Foundation Skills
3	Home and Neighborhood: Home	Filling out forms	Understanding simple street addresses; identifying name, city, and address on a simple form; matching words and pictures; copying and writing phone numbers and addresses	Identifying; requesting information	Foundation Skills
4	Transportation and Travel: Directions	Getting to know your town	Understanding simple directions and spatial orientation; sight word recognition; matching numbers and quantities; identifying room numbers and sequence on a simple diagram; understanding numbers 21–30	Identifying; asking for clarification; requesting information	Foundation Skills
5	People and Machines: Time	U.S. attitudes toward time	Understanding time and reading clocks; reading signs with business hours indicated; reading analog clocks; understanding numbers 31–60	Showing gratitude; telling time	Foundation Skills
6	Home and Neighborhood: Family	Sharing family information	Understanding words for family members; identifying family members and talking about family; reading simple biographical information forms; copying personal information onto a simple form; numbers in the tens, from 10 to 100	Identifying; demonstrating	Foundation Skills
7	Employment and Opportunity: Jobs	Mini-résumés	Understanding job titles; identifying job titles, times, and phone numbers in simple job ads; sight word recognition; reading the year in figures; recognition of work signs	Expressing state of being	Foundation Skills
8	Consumer Economics: Money	Shopping	Reading prices and price tags; reading symbols for dollars and cents; identifying amounts on coins and paper money; relating prices to coins and bills; adding and subtracting amounts of money	Requesting information; expressing gratitude	Foundation Skills
9	Healthy Living: Food	Groceries	Identifying food items; reading names of food items; reading labels and ads for food; writing prices	Requesting information; giving information	Foundation Skills

Scope and Sequence: Book I

Unit	Topics	Culture Focus	Functions	Grammar	SCANS Competencies
Introductory	Numbers; alphabet	Missing people	Greetings; taking leave; asking for information	Simple commands	Foundation Skills: listening, speaking, reading, writing
1	Human Relations: occupations; place of origin; filling out forms; giving personal information	Family and relatives; a family tree	Asking for information; introductions; giving personal information	*Be*: present affirmative and negative statements and contractions; subject pronouns; *be + from*	Work with cultural diversity; interpret and communicate information
2	Employment and Opportunity: applying for a job; jobs and activities	Supervisors and levels of organization; organization charts	Expressing needs; asking for information, giving answers; making offers	Present of *be*, yes/no questions, short answers; singular and plural nouns; *this* and *that*	Understand systems; organize and maintain information
3	Community Services: school and community; drugs in schools; U.S. drug, alcohol, and nicotine use	Volunteer and community workers	Telling about people; expressing wants	Possessive adjectives; prepositions of place; affirmative and negative commands	Teach others; allocate human resources
4	Home and Neighborhood: neighbors; helping people; child care and babysitters; child care coops	Neighbors helping each other	Refusals; telling about activities; asking for clarification	Present continuous statements and yes/no questions, short answers	Allocate time; negotiate
5	Healthy Living: healthy food; the food pyramid; fast food; planning healthy food	Fast food in the United States	Expressing likes and dislikes; ordering; expressing disagreement; expressing needs	Simple present, affirmative and negative; yes/no questions and short answers	Improve and design systems; participate as a member of a team
6	Transportation and Travel: travel by car, road signs, colors of cars; car maintenance	The importance of cars in the United States	Expressing likes and dislikes; apologizing; asking for information	Wh-questions with *be*; introductory *It*; information questions with simple present	Allocate money; interpret and communicate information
7	Consumer Economics: paying bills; job experience and office skills; wages, salaries, and raises	Minimum wage in the United States	Asking for suggestions; making suggestions; talking about ability and inability	*Can*, affirmative, yes/no questions and short answers; prepositions of time	Allocate human resources; exercise leadership
8	Arts and Entertainment: sports; cable and network television; amount of TV people watch per week	Cable and network television	Giving information and asking for information about the past; speculating about the past; expressing dissatisfaction	*Be*, past, affirmative and negative statements, yes/no questions and short answers	Acquire and evaluate information
9	History and Geography: famous women in U.S. history; Susan B. Anthony; voting	Mary Lyon, who founded Mt. Holyoke	Complimenting; talking about past activities	Simple past (statements, yes/no questions, short answers, information questions)	Organize and maintain information; understand systems
10	People and Machines: phones and phone cards; ATM cards; international calls	Smart cards with computer chips	Talking about plans; expressing necessity; making suggestions; talking about possibility	Future with *going to*: statements, yes/no questions, short answers, information questions; compound sentences	Monitor and correct performance; teach others

Scope and Sequence: Book 2

Unit	Topics	Culture Focus	Functions	Grammar	SCANS Competencies
1	Human Relations: school, company-sponsored training; elementary school, adult education	Asking for clarification on the job	Asking for and giving information; asking for and giving directions; introductions	Present of *be* in affirmative / negative statements, questions; past of *be*; possessives	Work with diversity; sociability, understand organizational systems
2	Arts and Entertainment: relaxation and leisure; going to the zoo; activity schedule, being busy, stress on the job	Stress on the job	Comparing and contrasting; giving advice; talking about preferences; talking about plans; arguing pros and cons	Simple present; verb + infinitive; adverbs of frequency	Allocate time; manage self
3	Home and Neighborhood: community problems; neighborhood; neighborhood security	Security guards	Offers, requests, and warnings; discussing problems	*There is, there are, there was, there were*; past regular and irregular verbs; prepositions of location	Solve problems; teach others
4	Employment and Opportunity: success and successful people in the United States; successful immigrant Americans	Teamwork and leading a group	Asking for and giving information	Simple past in yes/no questions and negative statements, past time expressions	Exercise leadership; monitor and correct performance; participate as a member of a team
5	Healthy Living: health, exercise, risk factors for heart disease; missing work because of illness	U.S. concerns about dieting and losing weight	Comparing and contrasting; asking for and giving advice	Direct object pronouns, future with *going to*, count and noncount nouns	Acquire and evaluate information; make decisions
6	Home and Neighborhood: renting an apartment; daycare; mortgage rates; renting vs. buying	Operating a home day-care business	Asking for and giving information	*How much/how many*; future with *will*; wh-question words	Serve clients or customers; negotiate and arrive at decisions; evaluate information and make decisions
7	Transportation and Travel: transportation; accidents and accident reports; trains and buses; buying a car	Driving rules and responsibilities	Asking for and giving directions; expressing necessity; reporting something	*Need to, have to*; present continuous; *could* and *would* for requests	Allocate money; demonstrate responsibilities
8	Community Services: libraries and community services; getting a library card; freedom of speech	Feedom of speech	Telling what one should and shouldn't do; apologizing	*Should* and *shouldn't*; demonstrative pronouns; demonstrative adjectives	Select technology; apply technology to task; apply problem solving skills
9	Employment and Opportunity: job search; interview tips; what employers want of new employees	Job search, interview tips, what employers want of new employees	Expressing ability and inability; making suggestions; giving advice	Meanings of *can* and *can't*; compound sentences, *must* and *must not, must* and *have to*	Organize and maintain information; sociability
10	Consumer Economics: shopping; discounts; bargains	Using coupons to save money	Complimenting; comparing and contrasting	Indirect objects; comparative adjectives; meanings of *could* and *couldn't*	Allocate money; participate as a member of a team

Scope and Sequence: Book 3

Unit	Topics	Culture Focus	Functions	Grammar	SCANS Competencies
1	People and Machines: business machines; the Internet	Machines and where they are used	Explaining; expressing needs; making suggestions	Adverbial clauses with *because* and *so;* two-word verbs	Select technology; apply technology to a task
2	Arts and Entertainment: U.S. jazz; music and clubs	Music festivals in the United States	Expressing likes and dislikes; asking for and giving information	Verbs with reflexive pronouns; *each other*	Work with cultural diversity; social skills
3	Home and Neighborhood: decorating one's home; colors; weddings; jobs in construction and design	Cultural connotations of color	Expressing needs and desires; complimenting; describing	Order of adjectives; prepositions of location	Creative thinking; acquire and evaluate information
4	Healthy Living: health, fitness, insurance; good and bad habits; longevity	Americans living longer	Giving strong advice; expressing possibility; predicting consequences; expressing obligation and necessity	*Should, have to,* and *might; either . . . or; must, must not*	Acquire and evaluate information; monitor and correct performance
5	Human Relations: family, personal relationships; Larry King; childcare	Changes in the American family	Sympathizing; expressing surprise; expressing agreement and disagreement	Past participles; present perfect with *ever* and *always;* object pronouns	Social skills; interpret and communicate information; acquire and evaluate information
6	Consumer Economics: food, ingredients, cooking; regional food products	Regions and the foods they produce	Expressing dissatisfaction; talking about plans; sympathizing; making requests and commands	Inseparable two-word verbs; count and noncount nouns; quantifiers	Social skills; acquire and evaluate information
7	Employment and Opportunity: job benefits, days off; work and home responsibilities	Companies and benefits	Comparing and contrasting; explaining; asking for and giving information	Comparatives; superlatives	Decision making; acquire and evaluate information
8	History and Geography: immigration to the United States; ethnic groups	Ethnic groups and their occupations	Expressing worry; congratulating; complimenting; promising; predicting	Past continuous; past with *used to;* future with *will*	Interpret and communicate information; acquire and evaluate information; work with cultural diversity
9	Community Services: animals and people; pets; types of dogs	Pets in the United States	Making suggestions; asking for advice	*Ought to, should, have to, must*	Responsibility; acquire and evaluate information; creative thinking
10	Human Relations: nonverbal communication; shaking hands; relationships with co-workers	Shaking hands American style	Expressing unhappiness; expressing desires; expressing possibility; expressing obligation	Verbs with gerunds; sentences with *and*	Social skills; self-management; acquire and evaluate information

Scope and Sequence: Book 4

Unit	Topics	Culture Focus	Functions	Grammar	SCANS Competencies
1	Employment and Opportunity: networking; writing résumés and cover letters; preparing for interviews	Job skills for the future	Asking for and giving information; giving advice; introductions	Present perfect; present perfect continuous with *for* and *since*; simple past; present perfect; and present perfect continuous	Acquire and evaluate information; identify human resources; understand systems
2	Transportation and Travel: transportation announcements; vacation requests; accident reports; travel costs	U.S. emphasis on driving	Discussing problems; asking for and giving information; reporting something	Reported speech; present perfect; past perfect	Interpret and communicate information; think creatively; solve problems
3	Home and Neighborhood: natural disasters; volunteer organizations	Volunteer work	Asking for and giving information; offers, requests, and warnings	Passive voice; present conditional, conditional with *would*; conditional	Participate as a member of a team; organize and maintain information
4	Healthy Living: medical insurance coverage and claims; nutrition; non-traditional medicine	Alternative medicine	Asking for and giving information; comparing and contrasting	Gerunds and infinitives	Acquire and evaluate information; solve problems; self-manage
5	Employment and Opportunity: citizenship requirements, forms, and exam; undocumented immigrants	INS rules	Giving advice; expressing necessity; making suggestions; arguing pros and cons	Modals of advice and necessity; short answers, tag endings	Acquire and evaluate information; socialization, participate as a member of a team/negotiate
6	Arts and Entertainment: opinions; arts programs; family plans; entertainment expenses	Dance in different cultures	Comparing and contrasting; describing	Present participles as adjectives, past participles as adjectives	See things in the mind's eye; make decisions; teach others
7	History and Geography: small business; job retraining; overfishing; protecting natural resources	Water pollution	Talking about preferences arguing pros and cons	Relative clauses with *who*; relative clauses with *which* and *that*; word order in relative clauses	Interpret and communicate information; participate as member of a team
8	Consumer Economics: banking; small business loans; budgets; saving money in the United States and around the world	Employee benefits	Asking for and giving information; comparing and contrasting	Direct and indirect objects, embedded questions and embedded yes/no questions with infinitives	Acquire and evaluate information; identify and allocate resources (money); interpret and communicate information
9	Community Services: community resources; community college courses; single parents in the United States	Parenting strategies	Asking for and giving advice; asking for and giving information	Time clauses; clauses of cause and effect; clauses of opposition	Acquire and evaluate information; solve problems, reasoning (cause/effect and opposition)
10	People and Machines: telephone bills; using answering machines and voice mail; technology in school	Technology at home and work	Asking for and giving information; comparing and contrasting	Future conditional; phrasal verbs and separable phrasal verbs	Participate as a member of a team; understand systems; acquire and evaluate information

Introduction

Program Components and Philosophy

Contemporary English is a five-level interactive topic-based English-as-a-Second-Language series for adult learners ranging from the beginning-literacy level to the high-intermediate level. The series includes

- Student Books for classroom use
- Workbooks for independent use at home, in the classroom, or in a lab
- Audiocassettes for individual student, classroom, or lab use and
- Teacher's Manuals, with reproducible activity masters and unit progress checks for assessment. These materials were correlated from inception to the California Model Standards for Adult ESL Programs, the MELT Student Performance Levels, and the SCANS (Secretary's Commission on Achieving Necessary Skills) Competencies.

Unique among adult ESL series, *Contemporary English* presents high-interest topics as a framework for developing a wide variety of language, thinking, and life skills. In addition to focusing on listening, speaking, reading, and writing skills, *Contemporary English* integrates work on language structures; problem-solving, critical-thinking, and graphic-literacy skills; and—increasingly important—work-related skills.

Contemporary English empowers students to take charge of their learning and to develop strong communication skills for the real world. For example, each unit in Books 1–4 falls under one of the following broad topics: Home and Neighborhood, People and Machines, Employment and Opportunity, Human Relations, Consumer Economics, Community Services, Transportation and Travel, Healthy Living, History and Geography, and Arts and Entertainment. (The lowest-level book, *Contemporary English* Literacy, addresses all of these topics except History and Geography and Arts and Entertainment.) In short, the series addresses topics of interest and concern to adult learners.

Contemporary English presents engaging and meaningful situations that provide a context for grammar structures, listening activities, and an emphasis on the world of work. Within this framework each unit offers a wealth of pair and group activities, often with designated team roles, and frequent individual and group presentations to the class. This approach mirrors the team organization characteristic of today's workplace and reflects the recent influence on education of the Department of Labor's SCANS report.

Teaching Suggestions

In general, keep the following suggestions in mind when you introduce activities from this series.

1. Rather than direct the classroom, try to manage or facilitate learning and encourage your learners to take active roles, even at the lowest levels of instruction.

2. Model activities before learners do them so that learners have a clear idea of how to work with a partner or a group.

3. Whenever possible, use students or classroom objects and people in your models. For example, say, "I am a teacher" or "She is a student." Move around the class and use gestures to convey meaning.

4. Review the directions orally and ask learners if they have questions.

5. Monitor learners as they do the activities.

6. Provide follow-up activities in some of these ways:

- When appropriate, post learners' work on the classroom walls for them to read.

- Have pairs or small groups share role-played conversations with the rest of the class.

- From time to time, have learners informally reflect on their participation by asking themselves questions such as these: "How well did I understand the activity? Was I a good listener? How much did I participate?"

As you progress through the units, always try to consider the book as a meaningful whole. Whenever possible, review aspects of content, language, vocabulary, and workplace skills, and incorporate them into each new unit. In this way, the process of recycling—a strong feature of this series—can be customized to meet the needs of your class.

General extension activities can be used in all units. In Book 1 you can use TPR (Total Physical Response) activities quite successfully as extension. True role-playing can be used especially from Book 2 on up. Improvisation can be used in Books 3 and 4. Strip stories can be created from the readings at all levels. Higher-level students can be asked to read or find newspaper and magazine articles related to unit topics. And for classrooms or programs with technological capability, the Internet, word-processing, database, and even spreadsheet activities related to series topics—such as job-search and citizenship issues—can be highly motivating and also practical, as students can list this experience for employers in their job-skills summary.

Use of monolingual English dictionaries is appropriate in Books 3 and 4, and bilingual native-language dictionaries can be used at all levels.

Dictations

You may want to do a dictation activity every time the class meets. Dictation is a good way to practice several English skills simultaneously, as learners listen, write, and read sentences in English. You can choose two sentences from one of the Scenes or a short section from one of the readings. Follow these steps.

1. Tell learners to listen to the first sentence but not write it.

2. Repeat the sentence. Tell learners how many words are in it.

3. Give learners time to write the sentence.

4. Repeat the sentence again if needed.

5. Show learners where to find the sentence in the book.

Language Experience Stories

At the lower levels of the series, you may also want to use learner-generated language experience stories in your teaching approach. If you are not yet comfortable using language experience stories as a whole-class activity, the following steps may be helpful:

1. Ask the class to look at a photo or illustration related to the content of the unit.

2. Have learners talk about the visual.

3. Write what they say.

4. Read their words to them.

5. Ask if they want to make any changes or corrections, but keep the emphasis on the connection between spoken and written language, not on correct grammar.

6. Read the story aloud while learners follow along.

7. Point to words and sentences and have learners read them to you.

8. Have learners practice reading the story as many times as they show interest in doing so.

Journal Writing

You may want to have higher-level students keep journals to improve their written English. If you have not monitored journal writing before, try following these suggestions:

1. Give learners a formal or informal schedule on which you will review the journals.

2. Tell them to write about anything they are interested in learning about that day or week. Low-level students or those who have little practice writing may need to write just one sentence every day at the end of class.

3. After reading each journal, write several sentences or questions about the entries.

4. Don't make corrections unless the individual learner asks you to do so.

5. Discuss journal entries with their student authors.

Bringing the World to the Classroom

1. Ask learners to look in magazines or newspapers for stories related to the unit. An alternative is to bring periodicals to class yourself and look through them together.

2. Listen to the radio or television for stories about topics related to those in the units. Ask learners if they have heard or seen the stories.

3. Talk about the stories in class and relate them to the unit.

Always encourage learners to take active roles, even at the lowest levels of instruction. One way in which you can move learning in a more active direction is to have students ask the questions provided in the unit-specific notes in this Teacher's Manual. You can write the questions on 3 x 5 inch index cards, hand them to students, and let them direct their own and one another's learning. Higher-level students can add a question of their own to the cards, and students can exchange cards. The possibilities for encouraging active learning with *Contemporary English* are unlimited.

Graphic Organizers

These useful tools for organizing individual or collective thinking and writing play a central role in *Contemporary English*. Graphic organizers such as Venn diagrams, idea maps, T-charts, and Johari windows can be used successfully in the learning process. Graphic organizers are particularly helpful in developing higher-level thinking skills, and the visual aspect of these tools makes them ideal for visual learners.

Even among experienced teachers and teacher trainers, there is surprising variation among terms used to identify certain procedures and techniques for language learning, so the following definitions may be useful to you in working with graphic organizers. Although you may already be familiar with the definitions, consider presenting them to your class and explaining that you will be using certain organizers throughout the term. In the student materials themselves, efforts have been made to provide very brief definitions in context so that students will feel comfortable with the designated organizers for their level even when working independently.

Johari window. A square divided into four parts; a four-paned window. While Joharis can, of course, compare four different things, they are most commonly used to compare and contrast two things in this way:

> panel 1: A has/does/etc. this

> panel 2: B has/does/etc. this

> panel 3: Both A and B have/do/etc. this

> panel 4: Neither A nor B has/does/etc. this

T-chart. A two-column chart (in the form of a T), used to compare or contrast.

Venn diagram. Two overlapping circles, also used to compare and contrast. Properties of two things or concepts are written in the outer portions of the circles. In the overlapping section, shared properties are written.

Idea map. An organizer used to brainstorm ideas and gather information. The map has a central circle with a topic word, phrase, or sentence and connected circles surrounding it in which related or subordinate ideas or examples are written.

Time line. Even at the lowest levels of English instruction, the time line is a useful tool for teaching sequencing skills. As your students do the time line activities related to the content of their books and workbooks, you can guide them, whenever appropriate, to create their own time lines for different stages of their lives. This process involves gathering data and subsequently organizing it and presenting it to an audience.

The Student Book

Before you begin the first **Scene,** discuss—or explain with words and gestures if necessary—the meaning of the title, which can be a springboard to understanding the central issues. You also may wish to bring in photos, illustrations, and/or realia that illustrate the content and the concept. At more advanced levels, ask students themselves to predict what the unit is going to be about.

Ask questions that encourage students to contribute general information and personal information related to the topic (for example, "Fatima, do many people have big families in your country? Juan, do you have brothers?").

Write some of the questions and answers on the board or provide a handout.

You may wish to have students ask and answer some of the same questions in pairs.

Scenes

Each unit is divided into two parts, each of which begins with a **Scene** that presents, in comic-strip format, incidents from the lives of newcomers to the United States or aspects of U.S. culture that students encounter regularly. Lively, humorous, and dramatic, the **Scenes** engage students in the unit topics—usually by presenting typical problems in the lives of average people. A series of discussion questions proceeds from factual comprehension of the **Scene** to personalization and, in Books 3 and 4, problem solving. For example, at the highest level the sequence is *Facts* (comprehension questions), *Feelings* (inference), *And You?* (application), *Comparisons* (often between the students' native countries and the United States), and, finally, the *Action* problem-solving questions—for example, *What should ___ do?*

Here are some techniques to enhance class work for each **Scene** with lower-level learners:

1. Write the conversation on the board.

2. Read or play each line of the conversation twice and ask the class to repeat it. Whenever possible, emphasize a holistic approach. In other words, try to have learners deal with whole chunks of language, rather than breaking language down word by word.

3. Read the language that learners have difficulty pronouncing and ask them to repeat words and phrases as a class as often as necessary. As soon as pronunciation improves, work with repetition of the entire line again.

4. Ask individual students to repeat the line.

5. Have students do a final choral repetition. Then move to the next line.

6. As each new line is practiced, add it to the previously learned section of the Scene. Continue this way until students can repeat the entire dialogue. At higher levels you may wish to have learners read the cartoon in groups of twos or threes.

7. Review new or difficult vocabulary.

8. Say the words and have learners repeat them.

9. Elicit definitions of the words. Check comprehension. If students cannot define the words, you can provide definitions or examples.

10 Extend the **Scene** by doing some or all of the following activities:

- Have learners spell the words (on the board or aloud).

- Use the words in two or three sentences.

- Ask learners to use the words in sentences.

- Have students practice in pairs as you move around the classroom, checking pronunciation.

- Have learners take roles and read the dialogue aloud. Allow several pairs or groups of students to present each **Scene** for the class.

- Have partners take turns dictating the conversations. Student A can dictate while Student B writes the conversation in his or her ESL notebook.

- Write three to five sentences on small paper strips and hand these to individual learners. When prompted, each learner can read his or her sentence. You can then write each on the board or on an overhead transparency. Lower-level classes can copy the sentences. The class can then order the sentences chronologically by assigning a number to each one.

- Read a summary of the **Scene.** Then write it on the board or an overhead transparency, or provide it on a handout. Remove the summary and have learners write their own.

- After learners answer the questions under the **Scene,** have each one write one or two additional questions to ask other learners.

- Have students retell the story and write about the pictures in their own words.

These activities are particularly useful with multilevel classes. The **Scenes** introduce students to the topic of the unit, give them a context for the grammar, get them interested and involved in the story, and build a context for the unit.

Sound Bites

After each opening **Scene** comes **Sound Bites,** a focused listening task that includes prelistening and postlistening work. **Sound Bites** presents target content and language structures through lively conversations and other samples of natural speech, such as telephone answering-machine messages and transportation announcements.

For any **Sound Bites** activity, you can follow these steps:

1. Read the directions aloud.
2. Model the directions.
3. Tell students what kind of conversations or passages they will listen to.
4. Read or play the tape for each individual **Sound Bites** item several times. Speak at a normal speed. Remember that learners don't need to understand every word to get meaning.
5. Model the appropriate written response.
6. Let students listen as often as they want.

At lower levels let students direct their learning by frequently asking them questions such as "Do you need to listen again?" and teaching them to ask clarification questions such as "Can you repeat number six?" At higher levels you may wish to have students take notes as they listen.

You can provide repeated active-listening experiences for all levels of students by assigning a different focus for each one. For example, play **Sound Bites** the first time and ask students, "Have you heard anything like this before? Where were you?" Then play the tape again and have students listen for vocabulary. A third time they can listen for something else—perhaps to complete the task or to listen for specific questions you provide, such as "What kind of person is Jerry?" Encourage students to compare answers. As an extension activity, later in the unit, you may wish to make the **Sound Bites** into a cloze exercise, for example, by leaving out the examples of the grammar point throughout.

Vocabulary Prompts, Your Turn, and In Your Experience

Vocabulary Prompts, Your Turn, and **In Your Experience** occur within the units at the point of need, rather than in a fixed or unvarying part of each unit. **Vocabulary Prompts,** for example, serves to isolate challenging vocabulary before a listening or reading task. **Your Turn,** a follow-up to reading, listening, or structure practice, serves as a participatory task. **In Your Experience,** an activity drawing on students' prior knowledge and personal lives, allows learners to personalize the topics and relate them to their own experience.

In Book 1, before students actually open their books to one of these vocabulary sections, you may want to prepare them by doing the following:

1. Show related pictures, maps, and realia.
2. Provide clear pronunciation models and ask students to repeat each word or term several times.
3. Provide additional explanations and examples as needed and use people and objects in the classroom whenever possible.
4. Finally, preview the **Sound Bites** tape and ask learners to listen for the words in the **Vocabulary Prompts** box.

A way to maximize learners' opportunities to practice oral communication in the **Your Turn** and **In Your Experience** sections is to use three-way interviews. These proceed in the following way: Students 1 and 2 talk to each other; Students 3 and 4 talk to each other. Then 1 and 3 talk, and 2 and 4 talk. Finally, 1 and 4 talk, and 2 and 3 talk. You can then assign all students with one number to report their results to the class. This procedure allows everybody plenty of opportunities to talk.

Spotlight

Throughout *Contemporary English*, grammar structures are first contextualized in the **Scenes** and listening activities, and then presented, practiced, and applied on follow-up **Spotlight** pages. Appearing two to four times in each unit, the **Spotlight** pages model target structures in contexts related to the unit topic. Special **Spotlight** feature boxes present the target structures schematically and provide brief, straightforward explanations when necessary. Exercises following the structure presentations allow students to manipulate the structures in meaningful contexts, such as stories or real-life situations. **Spotlight** pages usually end with a **Your Turn** and/or an **In Your Experience** activity providing communicative application of the new structures.

To present the **Spotlight** structures most effectively to learners using Books 1 and 2 of the series, try the following sequence of steps:

1. Ask questions that either lead into the target structures or contain the target structures. For example, to lead into the target structures, you can ask questions that would normally take an answer with the target structure. You can then elicit the correct structure or, if students are unable to produce it, provide a sentence containing the structure. In this way, you will establish an appropriate context for the target structure from the beginning.

2. Guide students through the language forms in the **Spotlight** box.

3. Elicit and answer any questions learners may have.

4. Provide oral practice for correct pronunciation of the sentences containing the forms.

5. Read any rules that follow the example sentences, and then return to the sentences to demonstrate those rules.

With learners using Books 3 and 4, the following suggestions may help:

1. Ask questions that either lead into the target structures or contain the target structures. For example, to lead into the target structures, you can ask questions that would normally take an answer with the target structure. You can then elicit the correct structure or, if students are unable to produce it, provide a sentence containing the structure. In this way, you will establish an appropriate context for the target structure from the beginning.

2. After you have elicited or provided several examples of the target structure, try to elicit rules from learners. Many may have encountered the structures before or may actually have studied them formally.

3. You may wish to put sentences on the board for students to complete with the target structures. You can continue in this way until the class begins to get a feeling for the new structure.

4. Draw two faces. Write a conversation in speech bubbles for them but leave blanks. Say, "Just shout out the missing part. What should it be?" (For example, "I want to _____." or "I need to _____.")

5. Have students open their books and look at the **Spotlight** box. Depending on the level and ability of the class, have students read silently, prompt different learners to read parts of the box, or read to learners.

6. Ask, "Do you have questions?" If no one has a question, ask students to do the exercises as suggested in the sections that follow.

Spotlight Exercises

Follow these steps with the **Spotlight** exercises:

1. Whenever possible, have learners do the exercises with a partner or a small group. This allows for interaction and speaking practice. Assign partners or, if the class interacts well without prompting, allow students to choose their partners. If some learners prefer to work alone, at least have them check their answers with a partner.

2. Read the exercise directions aloud to students and point out the completed example.

3. Model the activity and ask if learners understand.

4. Check answers by asking one student from each pair to read that pair's sentences to the class.

5. Allow for differences. Some students may be especially interested in learning forms and may want you to create charts of language forms on the board, on an overhead transparency, or on handouts.

Person to Person

Listening and speaking skills are developed further in the **Person to Person** activities, which present recorded two-person conversations exploring the unit topics in natural, colloquial language. Students listen to conversations, practice them, and work in pairs to complete a final open-ended dialogue. Students can then present their new conversations to the class.

Have students listen first, rather than read, in order to focus on the meaning of each conversation. Read or play the tape for each conversation separately. Ask learners if you should repeat the conversations or replay the tape. Ask some general questions (such as "Who are the speakers?") to check comprehension. Have learners practice words and phrases after you. You may wish to avoid having them read at this point.

Have students practice each conversation in pairs. Then ask for volunteers to role-play each conversation. Reluctant students will be more likely to participate after eager volunteers have done so.

Some students may not want to do the final, creative conversation, and it is better not to force the issue. Instead, you may wish to have learners again volunteer to perform conversations for the class.

Try to check the conversations learners create before they present them to the class so that errors are not internalized by listeners. Of course, even after you check the conversations, presentations will quite likely have some errors, but resist the temptation to correct as learners speak. A better approach is to take notes on the errors and provide these to students later, along with positive comments on their performances.

To extend the **Person to Person** activities, have learners record their conversations on an audiocassette player. Then play all the conversations for the class. Also, you may wish to have learners write their final conversation. You can then put all the papers into a box and ask each pair of learners to draw out a conversation, practice it, and perform it for the class. If appropriate, ask listeners to try to guess the authors of each conversation based on content clues.

Reading for Real

Contemporary English helps students develop their reading skills and become motivated readers of English through **Reading for Real**, a page in each unit that provides stimulating authentic or adapted texts. With passages and realia that typically relate directly to the lives of characters in the **Scenes, Reading for Real** includes such real-life documents as a winning job résumé, instructions for office voice mail, biographies of real people, advice from the local police, and listings of music festivals around the country. Follow-up activities (such as **Your Turn** and **In Your Experience**) extend and personalize the reading.

Before beginning **Reading for Real,** try the following:

1. Prepare students by asking them to look at the pictures and the realia on the page.
2. Have them glance at the reading and ask questions such as the following:
   - What is this? (a bill? a résumé?)
   - Have you ever seen anything like this before?
   - Have you ever gotten one of these?
   - How does it relate to what we've been doing?
   - Why are you looking at this?
   - What will you read to find out?

Continue with the following steps:

Books 1 and 2

1. Read the text aloud.
2. Check students' comprehension.
3. Encourage the class to talk about the topic by asking questions.
4. Record ideas on the board or a flipchart.

Books 3 and 4

1. Ask learners to scan for specific pieces of information. With less advanced students you may wish just to call out words and have students circle them.
2. Tell students to read silently without stopping.
3. After they read, ask them to check a maximum of three words they don't know. Tell them you will talk about the words as a class later.
4. Emphasize to learners that things can—and should—be read more than once. Tell them that even the best readers don't remember everything the first time and that those readers reread difficult sections automatically.
5. Finally, stress that they don't have to worry about not being able to pronounce all the words at the beginning.
6. After **Reading for Real, Your Turn,** and **In Your Experience,** extend and personalize the reading. For example, after reading a brief résumé prepared by one character, students, with the help of a partner, use the model provided to write their own résumés. Partners then meet with another pair, exchange résumés, and make suggestions or corrections.

Culture Corner

Culture Corner provides further work on reading skills by focusing on the useful inside information about U.S. life that students love. Presented as brief readings typically paired with charts, graphics, or artwork, **Culture Corner** gives students the information they need to adapt to a culture that can often be confusing and difficult to understand. Interactive follow-up activities help students integrate cultural knowledge with their language skills.

The following steps will be useful in implementing **Culture Corner:**

1. Have students look at the illustration or diagram.
2. Ask questions that encourage thoughtful guessing. If some students are advanced enough to ask others questions, encourage them to do so.
3. Have learners read the short text silently on their own.
4. When students finish, read the text aloud to them and check their comprehension.
5. Ask learners to create one or two questions about the text and ask a partner those questions.
6. If possible, have the pairs of students write their questions and answers.

As an extension activity for the **Culture Corner,** you may wish to do the following, at least in some units: Draw a simple T-chart or Venn diagram on the board or distribute copies of one of these generic organizer masters as a handout. Then ask students to compare some aspect of life in the United States to life in their native countries.

Scene 2

The second half of the unit begins with a second **Scene,** which usually reintroduces at least one character from the previous **Scene.** This is followed by a second, smaller **Sound Bites** that recycles the **Scene's** language and content. Next comes one or more **Spotlight** pages.

To recycle language effectively, before you start work on Scene 2, revisit the first page of the unit and retell the story in the first **Scene.** This recycling is especially important in situations where attendance is sporadic or where open-entry/open-exit policies are common practice.

Based on this rereading, ask learners to make predictions about **Scene 2.** Read the speech bubbles, look at the pictures, and follow the steps suggested for **Scene 1** on pages xii and xiii.

The second, smaller **Sound Bites** (which appears in Books 2–4) recycles the language and content of **Scene 2.** It differs from the first **Sound Bites,** which serves as an initial introduction of the unit topic in that there are no picture cues and students need to take notes on what they hear.

Get Graphic

Graphic literacy is the focus of **Get Graphic,** a feature that offers practice in reading charts, graphs, diagrams, and time lines—skills that are crucial in the workplace and for preparing for the GED. **Get Graphic** provides high-interest stimuli related to the unit topics and characters while it incorporates or recycles target language structures. A typical feature of this page is a follow-up activity in which learners develop their own simple graphs or charts and share them with partners or groups. The activities on this page help students learn to read, interpret, and use information in a graphic format.

Follow the steps below to ensure learners' success with chart and graph work:

1. Try to introduce the activity through something in the classroom. For example, if the graphic in the student book is a pie graph, use the board or an overhead transparency to draw a very simple pie graph for the class population with information about students from different countries, students' native languages, different eye colors, and so on. Explain what the graph is and what it shows.
2. Check students' comprehension by asking if there are questions. Also, ask questions about the information on the graph. If students demonstrate comprehension, move into the graph in the book.

3. Have students quickly look at the graph. Ask, "What is this? What is the title? What do the numbers on the sides mean?"

4. Ask if students have seen a graph like this before and, if so, where? Was it at work? in a newspaper or magazine? in a math class?

5. You may wish to discuss and demonstrate the meaning of words such as *axis, fraction, decimal,* and *time line.*

6. Finally, read the directions, point out any examples, and model the activity.

7. Encourage work in pairs and small groups. If students work alone, try to have them check their answers with a partner or a small group.

Issues and Answers

Problem-solving and critical-thinking skills are developed further in **Issues and Answers.** This feature typically presents two opinions—often in direct opposition—in formats such as advice columns or letters to the editor. **Issues and Answers** contains short, humorous texts with views of U.S. life from a variety of perspectives, including those of immigrants and their "cultural advisors"—the experts who help to orient the newcomers as they bridge the gap between their native and adopted countries.

Here are some ways to implement **Issues and Answers:**

1. Before your students read, have copies of newspaper advice columns available for them to look at.

2. Prepare them for the reading by pointing out the column format. Show them that in the advice-column type of **Issues and Answers** found in some units of their books, the letter on the left asks a question that the letter on the right answers.

3. Encourage silent reading first because **Issues and Answers** is a reading activity. With lower-level students follow the silent reading by reading the text aloud.

4. Check students' comprehension by asking questions.

5. Have a class discussion about the topic.

6. Record students' ideas on the board or on a flipchart.

Wrap-Up and Think About Learning

In Books 2–4 the last page of each unit contains a **Wrap-Up,** a project in which students use a graphic organizer such as a T-chart, a Venn diagram, an idea map, or a time line to brainstorm and organize ideas and then talk or write in a group. Following **Wrap-Up** is the self-assessment activity **Think About Learning,** a final reflection task that asks students to evaluate the quality of their own learning on the major content points, life skills, and language structures in the unit. Students can thus assess what they have learned and provide feedback to the teacher, all of which helps to build a learner-centered classroom.

At the very end of each unit in Book 1 is **Think About Learning.** In every even-numbered unit of Book 1, this activity follows **Wrap-Up.** In odd-numbered units **Think About Learning** follows **Issues and Answers.** In each case, **Think About Learning** provides a way for students to assess what they have learned and provide feedback to the teacher, all of which helps build a learner-centered classroom.

Before administering the unit assessment, or **Progress Check,** always take time to study learners' responses to **Think About Learning** and systematically review points that need further work, ideally working both with the whole class and with individual students or small groups.

Unit Follow-up

After learners have recorded their progress, you may wish to talk about the following in class:

- what students thought was the most important thing they learned in the unit
- what part of the unit they enjoyed most
- other situations in which they could use the same skills and strategies
- other previously mastered skills and strategies that could relate to the content of the unit just studied

In the beginning some of this may be difficult for students. Remind them to continue using previously introduced strategies and skills as they add new ones. As they progress through the book, they will expand their repertory of learning strategies.

Finally, before moving to a new unit, ask learners if they would like to do anything different the next time. Try to respect these wishes by tailoring the instruction for your learners, thus giving them a real sense of directing their own learning. The learning process will be more dynamic if these possibilities for building on experience and creating positive change can flourish in the classroom.

The Workbooks

The *Contemporary English* Workbooks are designed for individual independent study as well as for classroom work. In the Workbooks, as in the Student Books, a predictable sequence is maintained.

For ease of use, the essential information in the **Spotlight** boxes of the Student Books is reproduced in the Workbooks. Each **Spotlight** is followed by a series of contextualized practice exercises, progressing from simple fill-ins to more challenging activities that ask students to use the target structures as they write answers to real-life questions about themselves. Answers to all Workbook activities can be found in the Teacher's Manual.

The **Read, Think, and Write** pages at the end of each Workbook unit for Books 2–4 synthesize skills presented and practiced in the unit in an engaging multistage activity. The reading is supported by pre- and postreading questions. After the reading, one or two activities ask learners to organize the information, usually with the same type of graphic organizer used in **Wrap-Up** in the Student Book. The final problem-solving activity challenges learners to apply the content to their own lives. Each unit closes with a brief questionnaire, similar to **Think About Learning** in the Student Book, in which students note what was most enjoyable and helpful in the Workbook.

Using a Problem-Posing Approach

Contemporary English stresses problem-solving and critical-thinking skills. Many teachers, however, may want to go beyond this framework to use a problem-posing approach, which focuses specifically on the lives of students and their own special concerns. While all of the topics in *Contemporary English* are applied to students' lives, using problem posing may help to make the connection with students' real concerns even stronger. The questions on the first page of each unit are an ideal place to begin problem posing, which involves the three following stages:

1. listening for students' concerns and issues
2. having a dialogue in which the class thinks about these issues
3. thinking about changes that people can make in their situations and suggesting a course of action

Key to this whole process is to make the discussion as learner centered as possible, so that students' issues and concerns—rather than the hypothetical or imaginary situations of characters in the text—become the focus of discussion. The text, however, can serve as a springboard for exploring students' problems since it brings into focus situations in which students and newcomers to the United States typically find themselves. Of course, students' concerns will often go beyond the context of life in the United States; and if you use problem posing, you will want to explore all of these concerns, to the extent that students find them important.

The Audiocassettes

All key listening components of each unit are available on audiocassette. These include the **Scenes**, **Sound Bites**, **Person to Person** conversations, and the **Listen** component of the **Progress Check.**

The Teacher's Manuals

The Teacher's Manuals give teachers additional tools to enhance learning and create an active, dynamic classroom. These include the general Introduction you are now reading for suggestions on using the approach successfully as well as unit-specific pages with teacher-friendly suggestions for preparing for, presenting, and extending activities. For ease of use, the unit-specific directions for a particular activity refer to a page of the general suggestions in this introductory unit. Many content questions that you can ask students at various points in the unit (to check comprehension and encourage application and synthesis) are also included in the unit-specific notes.

In addition, the Teacher's Manuals contain a variety of suggestions for adapting activities to the needs of multilevel classes. These suggestions are listed as Options, and they are signalled in the text by the following icon, placed in the margin:

At the end of this general introduction are two special sections: "Maximizing Results in the Multilevel Classroom" and "Creating a Work-Oriented Classroom." Written by teachers whose classroom and administrative experience makes them experts in those issues, these sections provide valuable information on using *Contemporary English* effectively in a variety of classroom settings.

Assessment

Flexible two-page **Progress Checks** allow a program or teacher to assess learning systematically. The four sections of these tests—**Speak or Write, Listen, Language Structures,** and **Content**—can be evaluated quickly to determine readiness to move to the next unit. The **Progress Checks** are largely self-explanatory and need no special instructions here apart from a word of caution on the **Listen** section. It is best not to read the listening script slowly to accommodate learners' developing listening skills. Rather, it is better to read each passage two or three times—but always at a normal rate of speed.

Activity Masters

Two reproducible **Activity Masters** extend each unit's learning still further. One is an interactive activity—a strip story, game, sequencing activity, or information gap—that practices language structures and reinforces content. This master can also be effective as a team-building, cooperative-learning activity. The other master— usually an additional reading or a graphic literacy activity to be completed individually or in pair or team situations— can also be used as part of the **Progress Check.**

Here are a few practical classroom management suggestions for using the **Activity Masters:**

1. Explain the general purpose of the handouts to learners. Tell them that the handouts will give them more language and vocabulary practice and allow them to share information and ideas with other learners.

2. If possible, copy the handouts on card stock so that they will be more durable and will last longer.

3. Store the masters in labeled envelopes or in a small standing or hanging file.

4. Handouts that need to be cut have dotted lines and scissors icons. Rather than cut apart your masters, whenever possible, have learners cut their individual copies. This will give them a more active role, and it will decrease your preparation time.

An additional tool for each unit is the Workbook Answers page, also on a reproducible master so that you can copy it for students if you wish them to check their own homework or one another's.

Maximizing Results in the Multilevel Classroom

by Elizabeth Minicz, Harper College, Palatine, Illinois

Everyone who has taught adult ESL classes is aware of the phenomenon of multi-level classes. The causes—among which are varying levels of education, disparate skill development, and open-enrollment policies—are further complicated by other factors which affect language learning, such as hemispheric dominance, personality, and sensory modality preference. Given all the challenges of a multilevel class environment, can ESL teachers rise above them to teach effectively and even enjoy the process? The answer is a resounding yes—if they have some practical tips and tools to help them perform the job.

First, recognize and accept the fact that you cannot always be all things to all students. That said, allow yourself the freedom to experiment with the techniques, methods, or "tricks of the trade" that experienced multilevel teachers discover through trial and error, and give yourself permission to fail from time to time. Some years ago, Tom Peters cautioned people in the business world to make mistakes quickly. This is sound advice for ESL teachers too; if something isn't working, try something else—immediately!

Below are some tried and true ways for you to use the realities of multilevel classes to your advantage. As you read them, you may have an occasional "Aha!" reaction—Aha, I can do that! Aha, I've done that! Aha, so that's why that works! In the end, there really is no magic answer to what to do about multilevel classes. You need to decide what works best for you, feels most comfortable, and best promotes learning. These things will always vary from teacher to teacher and class to class. Here are several approaches you should consider in using your students' variety of abilities to advantage.

Approach 1: Use a Variety of Grouping Strategies

How are grouping strategies in multilevel classes different from grouping strategies in homogeneous classes? Actually, the techniques are the same, but the purpose or intent is different. Using various grouping strategies in any class enhances learners' opportunities for practice. In multilevel classes, however, variations on grouping structures allow you to manage learner differences and abilities better. For example, separating learners according to language groups is a general grouping strategy, as are separating by gender, age, or interest. In multilevel classes, learners' abilities—which may vary according to the skill area targeted—also determine groupings. In multilevel classes, higher-level learners may be grouped together for one activity, and in another activity they may be grouped with lower-level learners.

In multilevel classes, whole-class activities can help learners develop a sense of community as they help one another succeed. They foster the "We're all in this together" feeling that temporarily overcomes individual differences. In addition, whole-class activities are confidence builders. Shy or timid learners can watch, listen, and "silently practice" until they feel comfortable participating more actively. More assertive learners can serve as role models, mentors, or tutors.

Despite these advantages of whole-class activities, if you always keep your class together, you can "miss" two-thirds of your learners because the activities are often too easy for one-third and too difficult for another third. It is important, then, to plan whole-class activities in which everyone can participate according to their individual abilities and to follow up with individual, pair, and group practice opportunities.

In *Contemporary English,* for example, the whole class looks at the pictures in a **Scene,** listens to **Sound Bites,** or reads silently. Such activities are followed by pair or group work, subsequent debriefing for the whole class, and, later, workbook activities completed at home or, if time permits, individually in class. Although in the **Scene** or **Sound Bites** all learners receive the same stimulus, individual responses will vary according to ability.

You will want to vary the pairings or groupings of learners from unit to unit, page to page, class session to class session. In homogeneous classrooms the purpose of varying groupings is simply to "mix up" the learners to avoid predictability and routine. In multilevel classes the purpose is to accommodate learner ability differences. Less able learners should have ample opportunity to work with more able learners, but not all the time!

Think through the purpose of pairings or groupings before directing your learners to work together. Arranging by categories or by assigning numbers or colors is common practice in both homogeneous and multilevel classrooms. But in homogeneous classrooms the results are random, while in multilevel classrooms you will want to determine the *who* and *why* of the groupings ahead of time. And sometimes you will want to let learners decide for themselves who they will work with.

If you are especially motivated or fond of challenges, you may have decided to use more than one level of *Contemporary English* in your class. If so, it's a good idea to begin each session with whole-class activities. Then plan to meet for 15 to 20 minutes with learners assigned to one level of the text while learners assigned to the other level(s) do pair, group, or individual work such as reading or writing. Finally, end by bringing all learners back together for a final whole-class activity. Although teaching from three levels of the series in your multilevel class is possible, two levels are undoubtedly more manageable.

Approach 2: Adapt the Textbook Pages for Different Proficiency Levels

This approach requires more planning time than Approach 1, in which—with the exception of using two or more levels of the series in the same class—the stimuli are the same for all learners, but responses vary according to individual abilities. In Approach 1 it is your standards that must change or adjust. However, in Approach 2 the stimulus itself varies according to ability level. This means you must create or adapt tasks according to the learners' proficiencies. For example, if learners have difficulty generating language to talk about the **Scenes,** you might pose a series of yes/no, either/or, or wh-questions for them to answer first orally and then in writing.

Another way to adjust the textbook materials up or down a notch is to look closely at the tasks learners are asked to do. For example, in some **Sound Bites** activities, learners listen and write a word or phrase. You may instead want give your lower-level learners several choices and ask them to circle or check the answers—since checking or circling are easier tasks than writing words or sentences. You can also limit the number of items lower-level learners hear or, conversely, increase the number of items for higher-level learners. When in doubt, let learners decide which level of activity to complete.

Here are some additional ways to modify activities for learners' differing abilities. For the **Person to Person** activities, you can assign more advanced learners all four conversations to practice and role-play. You can ask lower-level learners to listen to all four but have them choose only one to practice and role-play. Or higher-level learners may need the additional challenge of writing more than one original conversation in **Your Turn,** whereas lower-level learners may need to have the **Your Turn** structured more tightly, with specific questions and responses that you provide.

On the **Spotlight** pages have lower-level learners work together to complete the exercises but let higher-level learners work alone. Also, you may want them to act as your aides by helping you spot-check other learners' work.

As you teach from the series, you will discover on your own more ways to add to or reduce the language load for learners.

Approach 3: Structure Activities So That All Proficiency Levels Can Participate

Several kinds of activities can be particularly effective in multilevel classes. For example, you can provide learners with grammar practice by writing sentences and questions from **Spotlight, Reading for Real,** or **Issues and Answers** on sentence strips. Cut the strips into individual words, phrases, or clauses. Clip the words from each sentence together or put each sentence in a separate envelope. Give learners the sentences to unscramble according to their ability levels, with longer sentences going to higher-level learners and shorter ones to lower-level learners. These strips are worth the time you take to make them because they can be used over and over again. To increase the longevity of the strips, use cardboard or laminate them.

Activities involving sorting or categorizing and variations on vocabulary bingo are easy to prepare and provide meaningful practice for learners in multi-level classes. For each new unit copy **Activity Master 8-2** from the Book 1 Teacher's Manual, write the vocabulary words for the unit in the bingo squares and duplicate the page for learners' independent, pair, or group work. Then give learners scissors and have them cut out the word squares. Have them use these words for several sorts: words they know how to pronounce, words they know the meanings of, and words they can use in sentences. Otherwise, they can also use the words for alphabetizing practice. Or learners can scramble the words, put them in a pile, and take turns turning over a word, spelling it, or using it correctly in a sentence. The variations are endless.

Traditional vocabulary bingo uses an enjoyable format to provide learners with scanning practice. To play vocabulary bingo, use the same generic reproducible master mentioned above. Make the game challenging for different levels of learners by having higher-level learners pronounce, spell, and give definitions. Have lower-level learners simply say or spell the words.

In short, to maximize the effectiveness of *Contemporary English* in multilevel classes, you will need to be creative and flexible, and once you have found new ways to implement activities, share your innovations and successes with your colleagues!

Suggestions for Creating a Work-Oriented ESL Classroom

by Jan Jarrell, San Diego Community Colleges

In the last decade, modeling and practicing workplace tasks and situations have become increasingly important components of the adult ESL classroom. This trend—together with the related tendency toward increased accountability—has been prompted by three interrelated societal shifts: (1) welfare reform, (2) governmental pressure on educational institutions to link funding to outcomes, and (3) the changing nature of the workplace as described in the 1992 Secretary of Labor's Commission on Achieving Necessary Skills (SCANS) Report.

Brief Background and Description of SCANS

In the late 1980s the United States found itself playing catch-up with two booming economies: Germany's and Japan's. Comparisons of work practices in these three countries became commonplace, and as a result, many U.S. companies switched to Japanese-style management practices known as Total Quality Management (TQM). This approach coupled an emphasis on teamwork with quality control at the level of the individual employee. In response to these dramatic changes on shop floors as well as in boardrooms, the U.S. Secretary of Labor organized a national commission to identify what the new high performance workplace demanded from workers.

The fruit of this Commission was the SCANS report, which identified two tiers of essential workplace know-how: foundation skills and workplace competencies. Foundation skills include basic communication and math, as well as higher-level thinking, decision making and learning-how-to-learn skills. Personal qualities such as positive attitude, self esteem, and individual responsibility are also considered foundational. The higher-order workplace competencies include understanding and effectively using resources, technology, information, and systems. In addition, workers need effective interpersonal skills so they can work on teams, teach others, negotiate, serve customers and collaborate on the job with people from diverse backgrounds.

Continued study of workplace needs and trends since 1992 has confirmed the relevance, indeed the necessity, of integrating the SCANS competencies into the curriculum at every educational level. In order for ESL students to get and keep jobs even at the entry level, teaching the SCANS is no longer optional. Many ESL programs in states with significant second-language populations have partially or completely integrated SCANS competencies into their curricula to meet these new challenges.

Promoting Teamwork in the Classroom

Of all the SCANS competencies, learning to work effectively in teams is perhaps the most pivotal. Teamwork either directly or indirectly drives most of the other SCANS skills, and yet many ESL students have had very little experience working in teams in their own countries—either in the classroom or on the job.

The most obvious and pedagogically familiar way of promoting teamwork in the classroom is by integrating cooperative-learning structures into your lessons. According to Johnson, Johnson, and Smith (1991), cooperative learning can be distinguished from other pair or group work because it includes five key elements:

- **Positive Interdependence:** The success of each team member and that of the team in general depends upon the effectiveness of all team members. By promoting activities such as jigsaws, which, because no student has all the information, encourage sharing of knowledge and resources, and by assigning group roles, you can allow work in teams to emerge naturally in your classroom.
- **Individual Accountability:** Structure activities so that all students must contribute. Assessing both individuals and groups assures that all learners must participate.
- **Group Processing:** Regularly provide time for team reflection and evaluation.
- **Social Skills:** Through your explicit teaching, modeling, and reinforcement, your learners can learn to lead, build trust, make decisions, and deal with conflicts.
- **Face-to-Face Interaction:** If you physically arrange learners to facilitate active involvement with one another as they discuss, teach, encourage, solve problems and negotiate, you will enhance team spirit in your classroom. In cooperative learning jigsaw activities, for example, students master content in expert groups, and then return to home groups to teach the content they have learned and also to learn new content from their teammates. As such, positive interdependence, new social skills, and face-to-face interaction are built into the activity. Later, you can assess individuals on all the content and ask the different groups to evaluate the strengths and weaknesses of their group interaction. This allows you to build in the other two elements: individual accountability and group processing.

Team Roles

In the work-centered ESL classroom, you can assign individual team members workplace roles. For example, in a group task, each team can be comprised of a manager or leader, a secretary, a supply clerk and a timekeeper. The manager must make sure that everyone participates and may also present the group's findings to the whole class. The secretary records and reports the group's answers. The supply clerk makes sure each group member has the necessary materials and also collects and returns texts and papers at the end of the task. The timekeeper keeps the team on task by reminding members how much time remains for completing each activity. You can assign some or all of these roles on a class-by-class basis, or they can continue over a period of time. If students take roles for one or two months, you can periodically have "managers' meetings" in which assignments or problems can be discussed among the team managers who then report back to their respective teams.

Just like roles in the actual workplace, these roles are flexible, and the titles or jobs that learners assume can vary by project and possibly by geographical area or by preparation of learners for a particular sector of the economy. Having a secretary may be meaningful when many learners will be pursing an office skills track; similarly, the roles of recorder and reporter may be relevant for later involvement in community service projects. The choice of roles really depends upon you and the specifics of the business environment in your area.

Using the Reality of the Classroom

As SCANS and the workplace become more of an influence on classroom instruction, ESL instructors are often pleased to find that daily operations of the ESL classroom provide many opportunities for students to gain actual work experience. These tasks shift responsibility for the ESL class away from you and toward students themselves. In the workplace-centered classroom, you as the instructor become a facilitator rather than a performer or directive manager.

Classroom Management. You can assign many classroom maintenance tasks to student teams. Team members can check signatures on the sign-in sheet, welcome new students, erase boards, and straighten chairs. They can distribute, count, and collect textbooks and set up and test equipment such as overhead projectors and audiocassette recorders. You can ensure that this work is shared and completed by posting work schedules that indicate which teams are responsible for classroom maintenance tasks on any given week or day.

Students as Trainers. You may wish to identify classroom procedures that students can teach new members of the class. Examples of these procedures are explaining class rules, showing newcomers how to fill out registration cards, and demonstrating for them how to turn on a computer or load a software program. Peer revision is another excellent example of how all students can function as trainers for one another.

Solving Classroom Challenges. It's a fact that certain challenges arise all too often in the ESL classroom. Insufficient or uncomfortable work space, inappropriate first-language use in the classroom, teams' failure to fulfill their classroom duties—all of these may seem to be inevitable features of the adult ESL classroom. But instead of first defining and then solving these problems for learners, you can turn them into resources by involving your learners actively in the problem-solving process. School or classroom issues can be identified through an anonymous suggestion box or evaluation form. Then, in teams, students can list possible solutions to the problem, discuss positive and negative consequences of each solution, and finally choose one of these solutions, implement it, and evaluate the results either as individuals or in groups. After students implement the solution, the results can be evaluated either by individuals or in groups. As an alternative, try holding class meetings in which one representative from each team participates in a brainstorming session while the rest of the class observes and later offers feedback to the meeting participants.

Of course, other problems occur on an individual or personal level, and students need to be armed with strategies to handle them. When a technological problem such as a computer failure occurs, you can encourage students to troubleshoot by following an established procedure. You can also teach teams a process for dealing with interpersonal conflict without your intervention. For example, you can train students in a round-robin exercise procedure in which each team member has two minutes to talk without interruption about what he or she thinks the problem is. Sometimes simply airing problems in this safe way will significantly diffuse negative feelings. Following the round-robin, individual team members can also write their suggestions for solving the problem that has been identified, the team secretary or reporter can read the suggestions, and all members can then discuss them.

Emphasizing Accountability

Using Agendas. One easy way of keeping a class on track and modeling workplace procedures is to post an *agenda* at the start of each class. The agenda can be simply a numbered or bulleted list, or it also can indicate time frames for each activity. As each task is completed, you can check it off on the chalkboard and have students mark their ESL notebooks. At the end of class, you and your students can use the agenda to review what has been learned that day. Highlight any items that were not addressed and indicate when they will be included.

Checklists and Logs. Just as employees often need to account for how they spend time on the job, students can learn to monitor their own progress by marking checklists of skills, competencies, and objectives such as the **Think About Learning** chart at the end of each unit of the student books in this series. You may also wish to have students keep a daily or weekly log of what they study and accomplish.

Evaluation. Evaluation not only allows you to assess students' learning and interests, it also encourages critical thinking and decision making, two important SCANS skills. Evaluation can be formal or spontaneous, but it is an essential element of any work-centered classroom. It can be designed either to help the learner think about his or her own learning or to help the instructor quantify that learning.

On the formal end, instructors can prepare class evaluations in which students rate specific class activities on a scale. Students need to practice providing feedback because in the workplace they will often be asked to evaluate training they receive. Students can also grade themselves in mock performance self-appraisals. The **Think About Learning** component for each unit of this series can serve this purpose.

Less formally, you can also "check in" with students by simply distributing index cards at the end of a class period. On one side have students write what they found particularly helpful that day, and on the other side ask them to note what was unclear—or what they would like to study next. Finally, to raise students' own consciousness about the SCANS competencies, you may want to create a class poster of the SCANS using level-appropriate language or pictures. Then, at the end of each class, ask students which skills they practiced that day.

Classroom Incentives. Many businesses have an "Employee of the Month" award, typically for an exceptional worker, who gets his or her picture and biography posted on a special bulletin board. You can adopt this practice quite easily in the classroom by recognizing an individual student or a team each month. You may also want to present end-of-term certificates for attendance, punctuality, outstanding performance, "best suggestions," and so on. In addition, you can give letters of recommendation instead of, or in addition to, certificates. Students appreciate "to whom it may concern" letters that describe their strengths—such as being punctual or being a team player. These letters reaffirm the SCANS competencies, and students can actually use them to get jobs in the real world!

Workplace Language. All the suggestions outlined in this section provide students with learning experiences that can help them develop essential skills for the workplace. However, most of these strategies require systematic modeling and practice. For example, students need to be explicitly taught language to facilitate teamwork. They need to know how to agree and disagree politely, ask for repetition or clarification, and give instructions. For example, one of many employers' most frequent complaints is that employees do not let their supervisors know when they don't understand an instruction or procedure. As work-centered activities are implemented in the classroom, encourage students to use clarification strategies such as asking questions and paraphrasing instructions. By practicing the language that characterizes this new classroom environment, your learners will be actively preparing for the world of work. If you can help them to articulate these newfound skills to prospective employers, their chances of turning a job interview into a job offer can increase dramatically.

Organization of the Unit-Specific Materials in the Teacher's Manual

In the pages that follow, the teacher's material for each unit is arranged in the following order.

1. Overview

   A. Objectives

      • Skills and Structures

      • SCANS Competencies

   B. Realia

2. Unit-specific Activity Notes (with answers for student book exercises and indicators for when to use workbook pages)

3. Answers to **Progress Checks** and **Activity Masters**

4. Workbook Answers (provided on a separate, reproducible page)

5. Unit **Progress Checks**

6. Two reproducible **Activity Masters** (Note: teacher directions—in addition to the teacher and student directions that appear on the master itself—for some of the **Activity Masters** are provided in the teacher notes at the first point in the unit where the activity can be used).

Administering and Scoring the Placement Test

Allow 35 minutes for completion of the Placement Test. Use the Scoring Guide and the Answer Key below to score the tests.

Scoring Guide

Scores	Book	Level
0–3	Literacy	beginning literacy to literacy level
3–7	Book 1	low beginning level
8–17	Book 2	high beginning level
18–25	Book 3	low intermediate level
26–30	Book 4	high intermediate level

Answer Key

Part 1

1. d	2. c	3. b	4. a	5. c
6. b	7. c	8. a	9. a	10. b

Part 2

11. much	12. did
13. are	14. wasn't *or* was not
15. Where	16. were
17. Have	18. did
19. shouldn't *or* should not	20. am

Part 3

21. d	22. c	23. c	24. b	25. c
26. c	27. b	28. c	29. c	30. c

Name _____ Date _____

CONTEMPORARY ENGLISH PLACEMENT TEST

Examples

1. Complete the sentence. Circle the correct letter.

   What ___ you do in the mornings?

   a. do   b. does   c. are   d. am

2. Complete the conversation. Circle the correct letter.

   A: Are you from Algeria?

   B: Yes, I ___.

   a. is   b. are   c. am   d. be

Part I

1. Complete the conversation. Circle the correct letter.

   A: I took a vacation last week.

   B: Oh, really? ___

   a. Where did you went?   b. Where does you go?

   c. Where go you?   d. Where did you go?

2. Complete the conversation. Circle the correct letter.

   A: It was Alice's birthday last week.

   B: Oh, really? Did she get any interesting presents?

   A: Yes, ____

   a. Tom bought to her a beautiful lamp.

   b. Tom bought a beautiful lamp to her.

   c. Tom bought her a beautiful lamp.

   d. Tom bought a beautiful lamp her.

3. Complete the conversation. Circle the correct letter.

   A: Excuse me. ___ borrow your pen?

   B: Sure, no problem. Here you are.

   a. Do I   b. Could I

   c. Would I   d. Should I

4. Complete the conversation. Circle the correct letter.

   A: Can you help me? I need ___ box up there, but I can't reach it.

   B: Sure, I'll get it down for you.

   a. that   b. this   c. these   d. those

5. Complete the conversation. Circle the correct letter.

A: My car is getting really old.

B: I know. You ___ get a new one.

    a. would   b. may   c. should   d. need

6. Complete the sentence.

Have you ever ___ any repair work on your car?

    a. did   b. done   c. does   d. do

7. Complete the conversation. Circle the correct letter.

A: There are so many dresses here, and I like all of them. I don't know which one to choose.

B: Oh, I think this one is the ___

    a. better   . b. good   c. best   d. well.

8. Complete the conversation. Circle the correct letter.

A: Where are you from?

B: I'm from Spain.

A: Oh, I have never ___ to Spain.

    a. been   b. being   c. be   d. was

9. Complete the conversation. Circle the correct letter.

A: How is your daughter doing in school?

B: Oh, she's doing fine. In fact, she's ___ than many of the other kids in her class.

    a. better   b. best   c. good   d. well

10. Complete the conversation. Circle the correct letter.

A: You should stop ___ those boxes like that.

B: Why?

A: You'll hurt your back.

    a. to lift   b. lifting   c. lift   d. lifted

Part 2

Example

Complete the conversation. Fill in the blank.

A: _____*What*_____ is your name?

B: Maria.

11. Complete the conversation. Fill in the blank.

A: How _____ coffee do you want?

B: About a pound.

12. Complete the conversation. Fill in the blank.

A: Where _____ you live in your native country?

B: I lived in Mexico City.

© NTC/Contemporary Publishing Group, Inc.

13. Complete the conversation. Fill in the blank.

A: What _____ you going to do tomorrow?

B: I'm going to a movie.

14. Complete the conversation. Fill in the blank.

A: Were you here yesterday?

B: No, I _____ .

15. Complete the conversation. Fill in the blank.

A: _____ do you live?

B: I live in Miami.

16. Complete the sentence. Fill in the blank.

What _____ you doing when you saw the accident?

17. Complete the conversation. Fill in the blank.

A: _____ you ever worked in a bank before?

B: No, I used to work as a cashier, but that was in a restaurant.

18. Complete the conversation. Fill in the blank.

A: When _____ you talk to the boss about this matter?

B: Only yesterday.

19. Complete the conversation. Fill in the blank.

A: This letter says I've won a million dollars, but I have to buy some magazines to get the money. Do you think I should do that?

B: No, you _____ .

20. Complete the sentence. Fill in the blank.

I _____ never going to understand this tax form. It's too complicated.

Part 3

To answer questions 21 and 22, read the following ad.

SALE!!! SALE!!! SALE!!!
Peaches 10 cents each
Tomatoes 29 cents a pound
Red apples 5 cents each

21. You want to buy four peaches. How much will you pay? Circle the correct letter.

a. 10 cents   b. 20 cents   c. 30 cents   d. 40 cents

22. You want to buy two pounds of tomatoes. How much will you pay? Circle the correct letter.

a. 39 cents   b. 60 cents   c. 58 cents   d. 5 cents

To answer questions 23–25, read the memo and the story after it.

MEMO

TO: All employees

FROM: Mark

RE: Vacation time

Beginning in January of next year, Bestco Inc. will shift to the following vacation schedule.

Employees with up to 1 year of service:
1 week per year

Employees with 2–4 years of service:
2 weeks per year

Employees with 5 to 10 years of service:
3 weeks per year

Employees with more than 10 years of service:
4 weeks per year

Frank Malyszko started at Bestco at the beginning of this year. His friend Juan started two years ago. Right now, Frank has three vacation days, and Juan has a week.

23. How much vacation time will Frank have next year? Circle the correct letter.

   a. He will have one week.

   b. He will have two weeks.

   c. He will have three weeks.

   d. He will have four weeks.

24. How much vacation time will Juan have next year? Circle the correct letter.

   a. He will have one week.

   b. He will have two weeks.

   c. He will have three weeks.

   d. He will have four weeks.

25. How much vacation time does an employee get after 8 years? Circle the correct letter.

   a. one week

   b. two weeks

   c. three weeks

   d. four weeks

To answer questions 26 and 27, read the following memo.

MEMO

TO: All employees

FROM: James Ross

RE: Changes in Health Plan

Please note the following:

Those employees who now have REGNA Health Care will have to switch to a new company. Employees will be able to choose between HealthPrev Company, Keystone Health Maintenance, and Arbco Health. Here are the costs for each of these plans:

HealthPrev Company	Family Plan:	$205.00/month for a family with children
	Joint Plan:	$140.00/month for a couple without children
	Single Plan:	$105.00/month for a single employee
Keystone Health	Family Plan:	$180.00/month for a family with children
	Joint Plan:	$150.00/month for a couple without children
	Single Plan:	$90.00/month for a single employee
Arbco Health	Family Plan:	$200.00/month for a family with children
	Joint Plan:	$160.00/month for a couple without children
	Single Plan:	$80.00/month for a single employee

Employees who currently have the REGNA plan may wish to discuss it with other employees who already have one of the other three plans above.

26. Which of the plans is the cheapest for a single employee? Circle the correct letter.

    a. Keystone Health

    b. HealthPrev Company

    c. Arbco Health

    d. They are all the same.

27. Which of the plans is the most expensive for a family with children? Circle the correct letter.

    a. Keystone Health

    b. HealthPrev Company

    c. Arbco Health

    d. They are all the same.

To answer questions 28–30, read the following passage.

What do you need to do to stay healthy? Well, diet and exercise play an important role, but an important factor is avoiding things that can hurt your health. For example, if you smoke cigarettes, you have a much greater risk of heart disease and cancer than nonsmokers. Alcohol can also increase your risk for these health problems if you have several drinks each day, for example, and it can lead to liver problems also. Doctors are unsure about the risk of having only one drink a day. Drinking coffee presents some of the same risks as smoking, but smoking is worse for you. Doctors caution us to keep our consumption of caffeine low, but many Americans drink three or four cups of coffee a day, or more.

28. Which of the following health problems is not mentioned in the passage above?

    a. heart disease

    b. cancer

    c. diabetes

    d. liver problems

29. What are the health risks of having one drink a day?

    a. very serious

    b. heart disease

    c. unclear

    d. no risk at all

30. If "many Americans drink three or four cups of coffee a day, or more," which of the following is probably true?

    a. This is more of a problem than smoking cigarettes.

    b. This is not a problem for people who don't smoke.

    c. This is more than doctors think they should drink.

    d. There are no serious health risks in drinking coffee.

OVERVIEW

Objectives

Skills and Structures

Understand and talk about U.S. schools

Listen to and understand conversations about school

Read and understand signs at work and at school

Read a pie graph

Read about and solve problems

Use an idea map

Ask and answer questions using *be*

Ask and answer questions using the past of *be*

Use *'s* to show possession

SCANS Competencies

Work with diversity: Student Book, Scene 1, page 1; Get Graphic, page 10; Issues and Answers, page 11.

Sociability: Student Book, Culture Corner, page 6.

Understand organizational systems: Student Book, U.S. school system, page 2.

Realia

Student application form or registration form for your school

A sign or notice for a class at your school

A newspaper advice column

ACTIVITY NOTES

Page 1

Scene 1

Refer to the general instructions on page xii in the Introduction.

Preparation

1. Introduce the topic of this unit by asking students about schools in their countries and in the United States.

   - How old are the students when they begin school in your country?

   - How many years do students usually go to school in your country?

   - Do many students go to college in your country?

   - Do you have a child who goes to school? How old is your child? What is his or her grade?

2. Take notes on students' answers and save this information for the Spotlight on Student Book page 9.

3. Show the student application or registration form for your school. Ask questions such as these:

   - What is this?

   - What information do you write on the student application?

Presentation

1. Ask questions about the pictures in Scene 1.
   - Look at the man on the left in the first picture. How old do you think he is?
   - How old is the man on the right?
   - In the last picture how do you think the younger man feels? Why?
2. Have pairs of students read the directions and text above the pictures. Discuss any words the students do not understand.
3. Have students read the comic strip. With the class discuss any words students do not understand. Ask for student volunteers to explain word meanings.
4. Have students read the questions below the comic strip. Make sure students understand the questions.
5. Tell students to listen carefully as you play the tape of Scene 1.
6. Have pairs of students answer the questions below the comic strips, either orally or in writing. If necessary, replay the tape of Scene 1.
7. Call on pairs of students to share their answers with the class.

Extension

Have pairs of students role-play the Scene for the class in one of several ways. Bring in props or costumes to make the activity more interesting.

Option 1: Students can perform the lines as written. You can assign pairs or let students choose their own partners.

Option 2: Students can make a simple substitution in some lines (by inserting the name of their own school, for example).

Option 3: More advanced students can ad-lib a conversation on the topic treated in the Scene or imagine they are in the conversation with the characters in the Scene.

Page 2

Vocabulary Prompts
Refer to the general instructions on page xiv in the Introduction.

Preparation

1. To introduce the vocabulary about U.S. schools, sketch stick figures and school buildings on the board or on an overhead transparency, showing all the schools in the chart. Make a story such as the following as you draw:

   Samir is 3 years old. He goes to preschool. Kim is 7 years old. He goes to elementary school. Maria is 12 years old. She goes to junior high school.

2. To help students learn the new vocabulary, use the sketches on the board to ask questions such as these:
   - Who is in preschool?
   - How old is Maria?
   - Is she in elementary school or junior high?

Presentation

1. Direct learners' attention to the Vocabulary Prompts. Use an overhead transparency of the chart (or write the chart on the board) and say the names of the schools and appropriate grades for each type of school. Have learners repeat the words after you.

2. Explain *adult school, vocational school, college,* and *university.*

To check comprehension, have learners refer to the chart on page 2 while you ask questions such as the following:

- Samir is three years old. Is he in preschool?
- Maria is 12 years old. Is she in the 11th grade?

Sound Bites

Refer to the general instructions on pages xiii and xiv in the Introduction.

Preparation

1. Ask students if anyone has a roommate. Put the word *roommate* on the board. Explain the word if students do not yet know it.
2. Read the first line under the Sound Bites heading or have students read it silently.

While You Listen

Preparation

Have students read through the first two columns of the chart. Make sure that they understand that each person listed in the first column is talking about a person listed in the second column. For example, Chela is talking about her son, and Mohammed is talking about his wife.

Presentation

1. Tell students that they will hear several conversations. Explain that you will play the tape three times and that they should try to listen for the specific information in the chart. Tell them that they do not have to write anything the first time they listen; they will write their answers when you play the tape the second time. When you play the tape the third time, they will check their answers.
2. Play the tape three times. When you play the tape the second time, students should mark their answers in their books. When you play the tape the third time, students should check their answers individually.

After You Listen

Presentation

1. Have students work in pairs to compare their answers. Circulate among the students and answer any questions they may have.
2. Go over the correct answers with the class.
3. If necessary, play the tape a fourth time to clarify any parts that students may have found difficult.

Listening Script

1. Chela:	Hi, neighbor.	
Neighbor:	Hi, Chela. Your son is so big now. Is he in school?	
Chela:	Yes, he's at Sunnydale.	
Neighbor:	Is that a preschool?	
Chela:	No, it's an elementary school. He's in the first grade. He's 6 years old now!	
Neighbor:	My goodness!	

2. Mohammed: My wife is a new student at North Park Adult School.

   Teacher: Great! How does she like it?

   Mohammed: She likes school, but it's difficult. She's 42 years old. She says she's too old to begin school. But she says that if I can do it, she can too!

   Teacher: I'm happy to hear that!

3. Lin: I'm sorry. I can't come to class tomorrow. I need to go to my daughter's school.

   Teacher: No problem. What grade is your daughter in?

   Lin: She's in the 7th grade. She's in middle school.

   Teacher: Is she 12 years old?

   Lin: Yes, she's 12.

4. Classmate: How's everything, Francisco?

   Francisco: OK. I got a new roommate, Beto. He wants to speak English all the time.

   Classmate: Is Beto in school?

   Francisco: He's a student at City College. He's 23 years old. His English is really good. You know, it's hard work to speak English at home!

   Classmate: It's good practice, Francisco!

Answers to Sound Bites

1. elementary, 1st, 6   2. adult school (no grade), 42
3. middle school, 6th, 11   4. college (no grade), 23

Your Turn

Refer to the general instructions on page xiv in the Introduction.

Presentation

1. Have students work with the same partners as for After You Listen. Tell students that they should write four sentences for each of the rows in the chart. Have students read the example sentences in the direction line. You may wish to model the activity by putting words from the first row of the chart on the board and then writing the example sentences underneath to show how students should proceed.

2. Circulate among students as they work. Answer any questions they may have.

3. Go over the correct answers with the class.

In Your Experience

Refer to the general instructions on page xiv in the Introduction.

Presentation

1. Explain to students that they will now work in pairs and talk about the schools where family and friends study. They will tell their partners details such as the ages and grades of the people they talk about. Each student should try to talk about more than one person.

2. Model the activity by telling the students about some of your family and friends. Then ask a volunteer to tell you about his or her family or friends in school.

3. If you wish to extend the activity, you can have students tell the class what their partners have said.

Page 3

Spotlight on *Be* in Affirmative and Negative Statements and Questions

Refer to the general instructions on pages xv and xvi in the Introduction.

Preparation

Review the present tense of *be* by writing the following sentences on the board:

- I am a student.
- You are a student.
- He is a student.
- She is a student.
- We are students.
- You are students.
- They are students.

Presentation

1. Direct students' attention to the affirmative statements in the Spotlight Box. Then erase the verbs in your sentences on the board and write in the corresponding contractions.
   - I'm a student.
   - You're students.

2. Repeat the same procedure to present negative statements and questions.
   - I'm not a student.
   - Are you students?

Exercise 1

Refer to the general instructions on page xvi in the Introduction.

Preparation

Have students look at the chart on page 2 again. Review the vocabulary and check students' understanding of words such as *middle school* and *kindergarten*. Review *ninth* and *third* if needed.

Presentation

1. Have students work individually. Read the directions to the exercise.
2. Read the first question and the example answer or have a volunteer read them.
3. Explain that students should use pronouns in their answers, not proper names. Make sure they know which pronouns to use.
4. Circulate among the students and answer any questions they may have.
5. Go over answers orally with the class.

Answers to Exercise 1

1. Yes, she is.
2. No, he isn't.
3. Yes, she is.
4. Yes, they are.
5. Yes, he is.
6. No, it isn't.

Workbook

Workbook pages 1 and 2 can be assigned after students have completed Student Book page 3.

Page 4

Person to Person

Refer to the general instructions on page xvi in the Introduction.

Preparation

1. Begin by doing a quick assessment of students' knowledge of the vocabulary in the Person to Person conversations and signs. On the board write the following sentences and ask students to fill in the missing words:

   - The class that teaches people how to be a citizen is called a _____ class. (citizenship)

   - When I fill out papers to go to school, I _____. (enroll)

   - The time when students enroll in new classes is called _____. (registration)

   - The place where students listen to tapes of a language they are learning is a _____ _____. (language laboratory)

   - When all the parents go to school to meet their children's teachers, the night is called an _____ _____. (open house)

2. Check students' answers to the questions and then provide the correct answers.

3. Explain any vocabulary words that students have had difficulty with.

4. With the class read over the signs accompanying the conversations. Check once again to make sure all of the vocabulary is clear.

5. Ask questions about the signs to check comprehension. Here are some examples:

   - When is the language lab open?

   - Where is the open house?

   - When is registration for ESL classes?

Presentation

1. Read all the conversations and have the learners repeat the sentences after you.

2. Have learners work in pairs to practice all the conversations and fill in the last sentence of conversation 4.

3. Have pairs read the conversations to the class.

Page 5

Vocabulary Prompts

Refer to the general instructions on page xiv in the Introduction.

Presentation

After leaners have explained words they already know, explain the new words and then check comprehension by asking questions such as these:

- Which word means "worker"? (employee)

- Which words mean "I get more money for my work"? (pay increase)

- What is the name for the person who checks to make sure work is done well? (supervisor)

- When I ask the students to write answers to questions to make sure they know the lesson, I give a _____. (test)
- When you take a test and do well, what do you do? (pass)
- What is the name for the person who puts parts of a machine together? (assembler)

Reading for Real

Refer to the general instructions on page xvii in the Introduction.

Preparation

1. Ask how many students work. Then ask if they ever see notices for classes or training.
2. Review the terms A.M. and P.M. Check students' understanding of vocabulary, if necessary.

Presentation

1. Have students read the Reading for Real text.
2. Answer any questions students may have.

Exercise 2

Refer to the general instructions on page xvi in the Introduction.

Presentation

1. Have students work in groups of three to four students to answer the questions.
2. Circulate among the students and answer any questions they may have.
3. Go over the answers with the class. Students may not be able to answer in full sentences, but short answers will be adequate. In some cases a complete answer can be found in the Student Book.

Answers to Exercise 2

1. assemblers
2. computer classes
3. Tuesdays and Thursdays from 3:30 P.M. to 5:30 P.M.
4. Employees get a pay raise.
5. the supervisor

Talk About It

Refer to the general instructions on page xvii in the Introduction.

Preparation

If you have a multilevel class, you may wish to group stronger students with weaker students. If you have students from several language groups in your class, you will probably want to create groups of students who speak different languages.

Presentation

1. Have students work either in groups of three or four students or in pairs. Read the directions to the class and tell them to give their opinions to the classmates in their groups. Tell them that they do not have to agree but that they should explain what they think.

2. Circulate among the students and answer any questions they may have.

3. To extend the activity, you may wish to have a volunteer from each group tell the class about the opinions of his or her classmates.

In Your Experience

Refer to the general instructions on page xiv in the Introduction.

Presentation

1. Model the activity by providing answers to the questions for yourself. You may also wish to have a volunteer give information about him- or herself.

2. Have students work in pairs to discuss the questions provided.

3. Circulate among the students and answer any questions they may have.

4. You may wish to poll students at the end of the activity to find out what they have learned about their partners.

Page 6

Culture Corner

Refer to the general instructions on page xviii in the Introduction.

Preparation

Introduce the topic of this lesson by asking questions such as the following:

- What do people in the United States say when they don't understand what someone is saying?
- What do people in your native country say when they don't understand someone?

Presentation

1. Have students discuss the answers to the questions in small groups.

2. Have a volunteer from each group provide a report on the group's answers.

3. On the board write the sentences that are in the speech bubbles. Ask students in what other situations people use these expressions. If students are not sure, give an example of a situation for each sentence. For example, a phone conversation with an unknown person who speaks quickly is a natural context for either of the sentences. A conversation with a salesperson who is describing a product is also a natural context for either of the sentences.

4. Have students read the paragraph about speaking up. Circulate among the students and answer any questions they may have.

Extension

1. You may wish to extend the activity by polling students about situations in their native countries when they ask for clarification about something they do not understand. Put the following topics on the board:

- the steps in doing a job (at work)
- homework assignments
- directions to a place
- phone conversations
- prices in a store

2. Make a table with the topics above in the left-hand column. Put the word *Yes* over a second column and *No* over a third column.

3. In a class of less advanced students, you may wish to poll the class as a whole and write the answers on the board. In a class of more advanced students, you may wish to have students interview other students and note the information on their own charts. In a multilevel class you may wish to have the strongest students poll the other students and then present their information to the rest of the class. Write the results on the board as students report them.

4. Look at the results you have on the board. With the class talk about the differences in numbers of students who answered yes or no about asking for clarification for any given topic. Ask if there is any reason why students ask for clarification more often in some cases than in other cases.

Exercise 3

Refer to the general instructions on page xvi in the Introduction.

Presentation

1. Have students work individually to answer the questions.

2. Circulate among the students and answer any questions they may have.

3. Check students' understanding of vocabulary. For example, make sure students understand the difference between *say* and *speak*. Point out the expressions *pardon me* and *excuse me* and explain that they are used in the same way in many cases.

4. You may wish to point out the fact that some of the words will need to be capitalized when students fill in the blanks.

5. Go over the answers with the class.

Answers to Exercise 3

1. Excuse   2. say   3. speak   4. Pardon

5. understand   6. repeat

Your Turn

Refer to the general instructions on page xiv in the Introduction.

Presentation

1. Explain that students must complete the conversations with expressions from Exercise 3.

2. Model the first conversation with a volunteer.

3. Have students work in pairs to practice the conversations.

4. Circulate among the students and answer any questions they may have.

5. To extend the activity, you may wish to have pairs of students present their conversations to the class.

Activity Masters

Activity Master 1-1 can be assigned after students have completed page 6.

Preparation

Before you begin this activity, you will need to make one copy of Activity Master 1-1 for each pair of students. Cut out the sheet as indicated. If necessary, review Student Book page 6 with students to prepare them to speak up when they do not understand what their partner is saying.

Scene 2

Refer to the general instructions on page xviii in the Introduction.

Preparation

1. To introduce the topic of Scene 2, begin by doing a quick assessment of these feeling words: *happy, sad, tired, confused, proud,* and *angry.* Check comprehension by asking questions such as the following:

   - Maria just said good-bye to her family. Is she tired or sad?
   - Chela's son is a very good student. Is she sad or proud?
   - Lee arrived in the United States yesterday. He was on the airplane for 26 hours. Is he proud or tired?
   - Kim's brother is coming to live in the same city as Kim. Is she happy or tired?

2. Explain and give examples of each word that students do not know.

Presentation

1. Ask questions about the pictures in Scene 2.

   - Look at the woman in the first picture. What is she thinking?
   - Is there a teacher in the second picture? Where?

2. Have pairs of students read the directions and text above the pictures. Discuss any words the students do not understand.

3. Have students read the comic strip. With the class discuss any words students do not understand. Ask for student volunteers to explain word meanings.

4. Have students read the questions below the comic strip. Make sure students understand the questions.

5. Tell students to listen carefully as you play the tape of Scene 2.

6. Have pairs of students answer the questions below the comic strips, either orally or in writing. If necessary, replay the tape of Scene 2.

7. Call on pairs of students to share their answers with the class.

Extension

Have pairs of students role-play the Scene for the class in one of several ways. Bring in props or costumes to make the role-playing activity more interesting.

Option 1: Have students dictate to you what Ha is thinking in each picture. Write the lines on the board and fill in any language the students are missing. Students can perform the monologue as written.

Option 2: Students can make a simple substitution in some lines of the monologue (inserting their own name, country, and teacher, for example).

Option 3: More advanced students can ad-lib a monologue about how they felt on the first day of class in the United States, or they can imagine they are in the conversation with Ha about her first day.

Sound Bites

Refer to the general instructions on pages xiii and xiv in the Introduction.

Preparation

Read the first line under the Sound Bites heading or have students read it silently.

Before You Listen

Presentation

1. Have students work in groups of three to four students.

2. Tell students that the faces show the feelings *happy, sad, confused, angry,* and *tired.*

3. Have students talk about their feelings about school. Allow them to choose from the words provided in this section or use words of their own choice to talk about their feelings.

4. Circulate among the students and answer any questions they may have.

While You Listen

Presentation

1. Tell students that they will hear several people talking about school. Explain that you will play the tape three times and that students should try to listen for what the speakers are saying about their feelings. Tell them that they do not have to write anything the first time they listen; they will write their answers when you play the tape the second time. When you play the tape the third time, they will check their answers.

2. Play the tape three times. When you play the tape the second time, students should circle the answers in their books. When you play the tape the third time, students should check their answers individually.

After You Listen

Presentation

1. Have students work in pairs to compare their answers. Circulate among the students and answer any questions they may have.

2. Go over the correct answers with the class.

3. If necessary, play the tape a fourth time to clarify any parts that students may have found difficult.

Listening Script

1. Hello. I'm a new student. My name is Ha. Today I'm confused, but this is my first day! In this class students work in small groups. We don't always sit and listen to the teacher. We work together. The class is different from classes in my country.

2. Nice to meet you, Ha. My name is Leonor. I'm in school today, but I feel very tired. I started work at 7:30 this morning. My baby was sick last night, so I didn't get much sleep. My husband told me to stay home and relax. But I know I need school!

3. Hi, everybody. Hi, Ha. I'm Francisco. I'm sorry, but I'm a little angry right now. My roommate moved my things, and I can't find them. I'm at school with no pencil, no paper, and no notebook. I'm a little angry, you know? Excuse me, can I borrow your pencil? Thanks, Ha.

4. Hello. I'm Tam. Today I'm happy because I helped someone on the bus. And I helped him in English!

5. Hi, I'm Chela. Yesterday my daughter asked me to help her with her homework, but I didn't understand it. I didn't go to school very much in my country. I feel sad when I can't help my children.

Answers to Sound Bites

1. b   2. b   3. a   4. a   5. b

Spotlight on Past of *Be*

Refer to the general instructions on pages xv and xvi in the Introduction.

Preparation

1. Draw a happy face and a sad face on the board. Ask the learners to identify the feelings. Then write these sentences under the pictures.

   • I am happy today.

   • He is sad today.

2. Erase the word *today* from each of the sentences and write in *yesterday*. Then erase the verbs in the sentences and write in *was*.

Presentation

1. Explain any new words such as *worried, surprised, embarrassed,* and *afraid.* Write them on the board and give examples of each.

2. To make sure students understand the meanings of these words, give additional examples and ask the students to identify the feelings. Here are some examples:

   • Late last night, Rosa was home alone. There was a strange sound outside her window. Was she embarrassed or afraid?

   • Lee's wife usually comes home from school about 3:00. Yesterday she was late. It was 4:00, and she wasn't home yet. Was he embarrassed or worried?

Exercise 4

Refer to the general instructions on page xvi in the Introduction.

Preparation

1. Ask students to define *report card* and *bills.* Go over any vocabulary they do not understand.

2. Have the class point out the past time expressions. Make sure students understand that these expressions indicate the use of *was/were*.

3. Ask which sentence will need a plural verb.

Presentation

1. Have students work in pairs to complete the exercise.

2. Circulate among the students to answer any questions they may have.

3. Go over the answers with the class. For each sentence ask students if they think any other feeling word might make sense. Ask them to defend their choices.

Answers to Exercise 4

1. was tired
2. were proud
3. was surprised
4. was worried
5. was embarrassed *or* angry

Your Turn

Refer to the general instructions on page xiv in the Introduction.

Presentation

1. Have students work individually. Model the activity by writing a sentence on the board about a friend of yours. Tell students that you are writing about a friend.

2. Have students write sentences in their notebooks.

3. Circulate among students and answer any questions they may have.

4. Check students' sentences at random.

5. You may wish to collect students' papers in a portfolio.

Person to Person

Refer to the general instructions on page xvi in the Introduction.

Presentation

1. Read the conversation and have students repeat the sentences after you.

2. Explain that students will practice the conversation once and then make changes to it. They will add any information about their own situations that they can think of. The important thing is for them to talk about an event or situation in the past.

3. Have students work in pairs to practice the conversation and change it.

4. Have pairs of students read their new conversations to the class. To avoid intimidating students, who will be presenting their own ideas, try not to correct errors other than global errors (errors that affect comprehension).

Workbook

Workbook page 3 can be assigned after students have completed Student Book page 8.

Spotlight on the Possessive

Refer to the general instructions on page xv in the Introduction.

Preparation

1. Use the information from the beginning of the unit (page 1) when you asked students if they had children in school. On the board write sentences based on the students' answers (for example, "Ali has a daughter in elementary school" or "Maria has a son in high school"). Try to put at least four sentences on the board. Check with students to see if the information is correct.

2. Underneath (or next to) two of the sentences, write new sentences with the possessive form of the students' names (for example, "Ali's daughter is in elementary school" or "Maria's son is in high school). Underline the 's on the end of the names.

3. Elicit the possessive forms of the names in the remaining sentences. Have volunteers come up to the board and write the possessive forms on the board. Then either complete the sentences yourself or have the volunteers complete them.

Presentation

1. Have students look at the first line of the Spotlight Box. Read it aloud to them and explain that the possessive is used to express possession but can also be used to describe family relationships.

2. Elicit additional examples from students about their families or other students' families.

3. Elicit the rule about the formation of the possessive: it is formed by adding 's or s'. Explain that there are singular and plural possessive forms, that these forms have the same sound, and that the difference is one of punctuation. Have students read the examples and the pronunciation note.

Exercise 5

Refer to the general instructions on page xvi in the Introduction.

Presentation

1. Review any vocabulary that students do not understand.

2. Have students work individually to complete the sentences.

3. After students have finished the exercise, have volunteers read the sentences aloud. Remind students that the plural possessive is pronounced the same as the singular possessive.

4. Elicit from students which sentences have the plural possessive form.

5. Have volunteers write the answers on the board.

Answers to Exercise 5

1. Mrs. White's   2. Jan's   3. The new students'
4. The teachers'   5. Sara's   6. the parents'

Your Turn

Refer to the general instructions on page xiv in the Introduction.

Presentation

1. Read the directions to the class. Put the possessive forms in the example on the board.

2. Model the activity by using possessives to talk about someone you know. Write the possessive nouns on the board.

3. Have students work in pairs to talk about someone they know in school.

4. Circulate among the students and answer any questions they may have.

5. Have volunteers tell the class about people they know.

Workbook

Workbook page 4 can be assigned after students have completed Student Book page 9.

Page 10

Get Graphic

Refer to the general instructions on pages xviii and xix in the Introduction.

Preparation

1. If students are unfamiliar with pie graphs, explain that they provide a visual means of comparing a part with the whole.

2. Make an overhead transparency of the pie graph or draw it on the board. Point to the different sections and make sentences about each. If necessary, explain the terms *under 30, unknown, over 60 years,* and *50 to 60.*

Presentation

Check comprehension of the pie graph by asking questions such as the following:

- Are more students under 30 or over 60?

- Are more students 50 to 60 years old or 30 to 40 years old?

Exercise 6

Refer to the general instructions on page xvi in the Introduction.

Presentation

1. Tell students to study the pie graph. Ask them the following questions: Which age group is the largest? Which is the smallest?
2. Have students work in pairs to complete the exercise.
3. Circulate among the students to answer any questions they may have.
4. Ask for volunteers to read their answers to the class. Provide the correct answers and model pronunciation of the numbers if necessary.

Answers to Exercise 6

1. 39   2. 22   3. 11   4. 50 and 60   5. 60   6. 13

In Your Experience

Refer to the general instructions on page xiv in the Introduction.

Presentation

1. Have students go around the room and ask one another their age. Caution them that some people will not want to say how old they are. Those who do not want to tell their age can say, "It's a secret." Ask students to tally the number of students in each age group, along with the number of people who do not want to tell their age.
2. Circulate among the students and answer any questions they may have.
3. Have students report their results. Ask volunteers to make a class chart on the board.

Activity Masters

Activity Master 1-2 can be assigned after students have completed page 10. This activity can also be used as an assessment tool.

Preparation

1. On the board write, "How many years did you go to school in your native country?" Have students volunteer responses. Write students' answers on the board.
2. Draw a circle on the board and divide it into sections. Ask students if they remember the name of this kind of graph.
3. Explain to students that in this next activity they will finish making a pie graph about the students at City Center Adult School and the number of years those students were in school in their native country.

Page 11

Issues and Answers

Refer to the general instructions on page xix in the Introduction.

Preparation

1. Introduce the topic of the lesson by holding up a newspaper and talking about the variety of subjects covered—such as sports, government, other countries, and important people.

2. Show the advice column and explain it. Ask questions such as the following:
   - Do you have sections like this in newspapers in your country?
   - What kind of problems do you think people write about in the newspaper?

Presentation

1. Have students write their advice to "Afraid" in their notebooks. Check what they have written.
2. Have two or three students write their advice on the board.
3. Discuss the advice. Have students choose the advice they think is best and explain why.

In Your Experience

Refer to the general instructions on page xiv in the Introduction.

Presentation

1. Have students work in groups of three to four students. Ask them to discuss their answers to the questions. Tell students to select one person from the group to record the answers and another person to report the answers to the class.
2. Ask each group to report its answers to the class. On the board tally the results: the number of people who like working in groups, the number of people who do not like working in groups, and the number of students in the class from different language groups.
3. With the class discuss any differences in learning styles that become obvious from the results. You may also wish to find out which types of group activities, if any, students prefer. If students have specific preferences for group activities, you can follow up on this information by having them plan specific activities for future lessons. Students can work in groups or by themselves to provide suggestions for activities. You can then put the suggestions to a vote, or you can have a class discussion or further collaborative group work to continue planning, as you see fit.

Page 12

Wrap-Up

Refer to the general instructions on pages xix and xx in the Introduction.

Preparation

1. Introduce the concept of idea maps by drawing a blank one on the board. Follow the example on page 12.
2. Choose a topic and write it in the center circle. (Example: how to learn English.)
3. Fill in one circle with an idea about the topic. (Examples: go to school or watch TV.)
4. Ask students for other ideas about the topic. Write their suggestions in the remaining circles. Here is an example of an idea map:

Presentation

1. Have students work in groups to complete the idea map on Student Book page 12. You may wish to have students copy the idea map onto a larger sheet of paper. Read the directions to the class and explain that they should complete the idea map first and then make a list of their ideas. Have each group choose a student to make a list of the ideas and another student to report the ideas to the class.

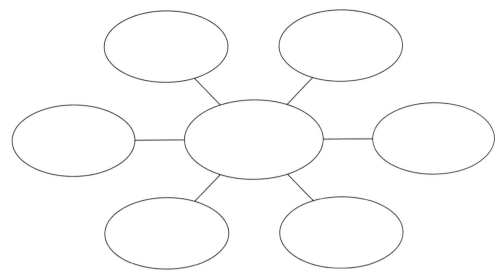

2. Have the student elected for each group report the group's ideas to the class.

3. If there is significant disagreement among the groups, you may wish to discuss the students' ideas with the whole class.

Extension

1. Have students make idea maps on topics of their own choice. Ask students to choose another topic, such as how to keep our school clean, how to meet new friends, or how to be healthy. They can work in groups to make an idea map on the topic they have chosen. This activity allows for two variations: either all of the groups can make idea maps on the same topic, or each group can choose a separate topic.

2. Check the students' work and invite a few students to write their idea maps on the board.

3. Discuss the idea maps. Have students choose which idea map they think is best and explain why.

Think About Learning

Refer to the general instructions on pages xix and xx in the Introduction.

Preparation

Explain to students that they can think about their learning in each unit of the book. In this way, they can monitor how much progress they make and the areas in which they think they need to do better. Students will thus have greater control over what they learn and will be able to give better feedback to the teacher about what is difficult and what is easy for them. Encourage students to fill in their charts and provide feedback about how they think they are doing.

Presentation

1. Have students fill in their charts individually.

2. Explain that they can look up the pages where they worked on a specific skill or structure. The page references are provided in the second column of the chart.

3. Circulate among the students and answer any questions they may have.

4. Encourage students to add extra details in the bottom row of the chart. If they do not wish to comment on something else they have learned, they can make comments about what they would like to learn.

5. Encourage students to share their responses with you. Make it clear to them that they will not be graded on this self-assessment.

Workbook

Workbook pages 5 and 6 can be assigned after students have completed Student Book page 12.

ANSWERS TO PROGRESS CHECK

Progress Check A

Speak or Write

1. Ha is afraid or nervous.
2. Ha is confused because the class is different from classes in her country.
3. Answers will vary.

Listening Script

1. Mrs. White teaches 6th grade.
2. Today the students are going to a new school.
3. Jan does not have her books.
4. Chen likes his teacher.
5. Sara goes to English class once a week.

Listen

1. Mrs. White's   2. The students'   3. Jan's   4. Chen's   5. Sara's

Progress Check B

Language Structures

1. Are   2. are   3. 's (is)   4. is   5. 's (is)   6. Are   7. aren't
8. 's (is)   9. 's (is)   10. 's (is)   11. 's (is)

Content

1. senior high school   2. 40   3. isn't   4. can   5. ask questions   6. together

ANSWERS TO ACTIVITY MASTERS

Activity Master 1-1

Answers will vary.

Activity Master 1-2

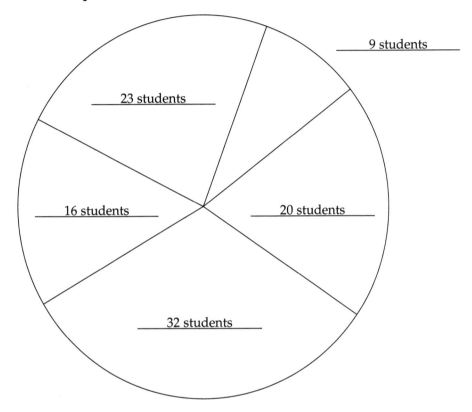

REPRODUCIBLE MASTER
UNIT 1

WORKBOOK ANSWERS

Practice 1

1. Are   2. not, am   3. Is   4. he isn't, He's
5. is   6. Is   7. is, is

Practice 2

1. No, he isn't.   2. Yes, I am.   3. Yes, he is.
4. Answers will vary.

Practice 3

1. Is Lin a teacher?

2. Is she in high school?

3. Is Lin married?

4. Is her daughter in the 6th grade?

5. Is her daughter in elementary school?

6. Are her sons in kindergarten?

Practice 4

1. Yes, she was.   2. No, they weren't.   3. Yes, he was.
4. Yes, she was.   5. Yes, I was.

Practice 5

1. Chen-Li's   2. Samir's   3. Christina's   4. Samir's
5. Christina's   6. Chen-Li's   7. Christina's   8. Samir's

Practice 6

1. Yes, he does.   2. high school
3. No, he didn't.   5. Yes, there are.
6. No, there aren't.

REPRODUCIBLE MASTER
UNIT 1

PROGRESS CHECK A

SPEAK OR WRITE

Look at the pictures from Unit 1. Use the questions below to talk or write about each picture.

Questions

1. How does Ha feel in the first picture?

2. Why is Ha confused in the second picture?

3. Think about your first day of class. Were you happy or afraid? How did you feel? Why?

LISTEN

Listen to the teacher. Complete the sentences below with the possessive form of the words you hear.

1. _____ class is in Room 19.

2. _____ new school is very large.

3. _____ books are on the table.

4. _____ teacher is from New York.

5. _____ English class meets every Monday.

PROGRESS CHECK B

LANGUAGE STRUCTURES

Complete the conversation. Use the correct forms of *be*.

Ha: (1) _____ your children in school?

Mohammed: Yes, they (2) _____. My oldest son

               (3) _____ at the university.

Ha: How old (4) _____ he?

Mohammed: He (5) _____ 22 years old.

Ha: (6) _____ your other children at the university?

Mohammed: No, they (7) _____.

               My daughter (8) _____ in high school.

               She (9) _____ 18 years old.

               My other son (10) _____ in junior high school.

               He (11) _____ 14 years old.

CONTENT

Underline the correct answers.

1. In the U.S. school system, a student in 12th grade is in
   (*elementary school, senior high school*).

2. A student in adult school is (*14, 40*) years old.

3. A student in 5th grade probably (*is, isn't*) 5 years old.

4. A person 70 years old (*can, can't*) go to school.

5. When you don't understand your boss, teacher, or other students,
   (*ask questions, be quiet*).

6. Teachers in the United States like group work because students
   work (*together, alone*).

Name _____ Date _____

✂ -

Student A: Ask Student B these questions and fill out the school registration form. When you don't understand the information, ask Student B to repeat or speak more slowly.

1. What's his last name?

2. What's his birthdate?

3. What's his native country?

CITY CENTER ADULT SCHOOL REGISTRATION FORM

Name _____Ly_____ Telephone _619-483-7121_
   Last   First

Address __1064 Elm Street, Apt. 3B_____
    Number   Street   Apt.

_____
City   State   Zip Code

Birthdate _____ Social Security Number _601-52-4719_

Native Country _____ Years of School __8__

✂ -

Student B: Ask Student A these questions and fill out the registration form. When you don't understand the information, ask Student A to repeat or speak more slowly.

1. What's his telephone number?

2. What's his address?

3. How many years of school does he have?

CITY CENTER ADULT SCHOOL REGISTRATION FORM

Name __Nguyen, Ly__ Telephone _____
   Last   First

Address _____
    Number   Street   Apt.

_____
City   State   Zip Code

Birthdate _9-6-46_ Social Security Number _601-52-4719_

Native Country __Viet Nam__ Years of School _____

© NTC/Contemporary Publishing Group, Inc.

Name _____   Date _____

MORE GRAPHIC SKILLS

Below is a pie graph about City Center Adult School students. The graph shows how many years students went to school in their native countries. The graph isn't finished. Read about the students below and write the information on the correct part of the pie graph.

Years of School in the Native Country of 100 ESL Students at City Center Adult School

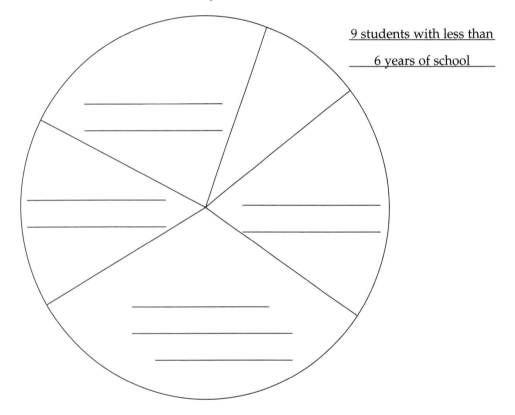

9 students with less than 6 years of school

1. There are 9 students with less than 6 years of school.

2. There are 20 students with 6–8 years of school.

3. There are 32 students with 9–10 years of school.

4. There are 23 students with 11–12 years of school.

5. There are 16 students with 13 or more years of school.

Unit 2   Relax!

OVERVIEW

Objectives

Skills and Structures

Talk about people's problems

Listen to map directions

Understand schedules

Read a bar graph

Present pros and cons of an issue

Use a T-chart and present ideas

Use the simple present tense

Use verb + infinitive

Use adverbs of frequency

SCANS Competencies

Allocate time: Student Book, Scene 2, page 19.

Manage self: Student Book, Scene 1, page 13; Student Book, Culture Corner, page 18.

Realia

Class schedule from local recreation center

Tape of relaxing type of music

ACTIVITY NOTES

Page 13

Scene 1

Refer to the general instructions on pages xii and xiii in the Introduction.

Preparation

1. Introduce this unit by playing a relaxing musical tape as students arrive. Ask questions such as the following:

   - Do you like this music?

   - How do you feel when you listen to this music?

   - Where do you usually relax?

Presentation

1. Have students look at the first picture in Scene 1. Ask

   - Where are these people?

   - Do they look relaxed? Why or why not?

2. Have students look at the last picture in Scene 1. Ask, "How does Janet feel now? How do you know?"

Extension

1. After the students study page 13, ask them to work in groups to discuss how they relax. Then have them share their answers. Make a list of their answers on the board.

2. Have pairs of students role-play the Scene for the class in one of several ways. Bring in props or costumes to make the activity more interesting.

Option 1: Students can pantomime favorite relaxation activities from the Extension Activity list on the board for their partners to guess.

Option 2: Students can make a simple substitution in some lines (by inserting their own weekend plans, for example).

Option 3: More advanced students can ad-lib a conversation on the topic treated in the Scene, or imagine they are in the conversation with the characters in the Scene.

Page 14

Sound Bites

Refer to the general instructions on pages xiii and xiv in the Introduction.

Preparation

1. Prepare the students for the map-drawing exercise by asking them about places they like to go in their community.

2. Draw a large rectangle on the board to represent their neighborhood, and sketch buildings, trees, etc., to demonstrate their respective locations. This "map" will serve as an example for students to follow.

Before You Listen

Preparation

1. To check comprehension of place names, ask students to name their favorite local version of the places listed. Clarify any words the students are unsure of.

2. Ask for a volunteer to explain the word *usually* and give an example. If no one can define it, say "If I usually do something, that means I do it most of the time but not all the time."

Presentation

1. Have students work in groups of three to discuss the questions. If all three students have the same answers for a given location, have them share it with the class.

2. Write those common answers on the board, and ask how many students in the rest of the class also do those things there. Save the information for use later in Get Graphic.

While You Listen

Preparation

1. Have students read over the place names in the map. Clarify any words students don't understand.

2. Point out that the word *artist* refers to a person, not a place.

3. Make sure students understand that they will be drawing paths for two people so they should use different-colored pencils to distinguish between them. Have some available for students to borrow.

Presentation

1. Read the first line under the Sound Bites heading or have students read it silently.

2. Tell students you will be playing the tape three times. The first time they should just listen for important information (such as place names). The second time they hear the tape, students should draw the lines. You may want to stop the tape between speakers to allow students to change pencils. The third time students hear the tape, they should check over their answers individually.

After You Listen

Presentation

Have students work in pairs to compare answers.

Listening Script

Narrator: Chan and Janet are talking about how they like to relax on the weekends.

Chan: I'm Chan. I really know how to relax. Let me tell you about my day at Himmel Park. I have a year's pass to the zoo, so in the morning I watch the animals. Later I meet my friends at the picnic area, and we eat lunch. Then we play baseball at the field for a couple of hours. If there's time, we listen to music at the concert area.

Janet: You were at the park yesterday? So was I! I love going to Himmel Park every weekend. First, I visit the science museum to see the exhibits. Then I walk slowly down the main road and watch the artist. For lunch I eat a sandwich at the picnic area. Sometimes I visit the art museum and look at the paintings and drawings. In the evening I walk to the concert area and listen to music there.

Answers to Sound Bites

Chan first goes to the zoo, then the picnic area, then the baseball field, and then to the concert area.

Janet first goes to the science museum, then walks down the main road, then watches the artist, then eats at the picnic area, then visits the art museum, and then goes to the concert area.

Your Turn

Refer to the general instructions on page xiv in the Introduction.

Preparation

1. If possible, have students choose one park and one shopping center that everyone knows, to minimize confusion.

2. Discuss the kinds of places people go to in parks and shopping malls. Make two lists of student-generated vocabulary on the board for students to refer to.

3. Provide unlined paper for students to draw their own maps on.

Presentation

1. Have students draw their maps and trace their routes individually. Give them a time limit of about 10 minutes. Then have students form pairs or groups of three. Everyone in the pair or group should have chosen the same location (the park or the shopping mall).

2. Remind students to use connecting words such as *first, next, then,* etc., when describing their weekend schedules.

3. To check comprehension, have group members trace the speaker's route on their own maps as she is speaking.

Page 15

Spotlight on Simple Present

Refer to the general instructions on page xv in the Introduction.

Preparation

1. Review present tense by asking questions about the students' usual weekend activities. Ask questions such as the following: What do you do on Sundays?

2. Write one or two sentences on the board, using the students' names and responses. For example, write the following:

   • José plays soccer on Sundays.

   • Maria and Marta go to the park on Sundays.

3. Use the information on the board and ask yes/no questions.

   • Lam, do you play soccer on Sundays?

   • Martin, do you go to the park on Sundays?

   • How about you, Chung? Do you go to the park on Sundays?

4. When students give negative answers, write sentences on the board. For example, write the following:

   • Lam doesn't play soccer on Sundays.

   • Martin and Chung don't go to the park on Sundays.

5. Explain that *on Sundays* is used to talk about things we usually do every Sunday.

Presentation

1. Direct students to read the sentences in the Spotlight Box silently as you read them aloud.

2. Explain any vocabulary students do not understand.

3. Elicit from students the rule that the verb form is the same for all the subjects except *he / she / it*. Ask for one volunteer to explain the difference in positive statements and one to explain the difference in negative statements.

Exercise I

Refer to the general instructions on page xvi in the Introduction.

Presentation

1. Have students read the chart individually. Ask questions such as the following:

   • How many people are listed in the chart?

   • Who does things together on Saturdays, Antonio and Gloria or Gloria and Marta?

2. Explain any vocabulary students do not understand.

3. Point out to students that the verbs in the schedule may have to be changed in the sentences. Have them compare the schedule with the first example sentence and tell the difference.

Answers to Exercise 1

Answers will vary. Possible answers include the following:

1. Antonio plays soccer from 9:00 to 12:00.

2. Antonio goes on a picnic from 12:00 to 3:00.

3. He goes to a rock concert from 3:00 to 5:00.

4. He doesn't go shopping, eat lunch, or go to the movies.

5. Gloria and Marta go shopping from 10:00 to 1:00.

6. They eat lunch from 1:00 to 2:00.

7. They don't play soccer.

In Your Experience

Refer to the general instructions on page xiv in the Introduction.

Preparation

1. Draw a blank chart on the board similar to the one in Exercise 1 for students to copy in their notebooks. They should fill one side in with their own activities and the other with their partner's.

2. Have students fill in the left side of this chart individually, including the day, before they pair up to talk about their schedule. They do not have to use complete sentences in the chart.

Presentation

1. Remind students to use complete sentences when talking to their partners.

2. As one partner is speaking, the other should be filling in the information in the right side of his or her chart.

Workbook

Workbook page 7 can be assigned after students have completed Student Book page 15.

Page 16

Vocabulary Prompts

Refer to the general instructions on page xiv in the Introduction.

Presentation

1. After students discuss the Vocabulary Prompts in a small group, ask for definitions or examples of the words. Explain any words the students do not know.

2. To check comprehension, write the following sentences on the board and have volunteers come up and write in the correct words.

   • When I come home from work, sit down and watch TV, or do nothing, I _____. (relax)

   • A small restaurant is a _____. (cafe)

   • A plan for the day is a _____. (schedule)

   • When I have free time to do what I want to do, I have _____ time. (leisure)

Person to Person

Refer to the general instructions on page xvi in the Introduction.

Presentation

1. Choose a volunteer to read the directions aloud.

2. Read through the conversations line by line. Have the students repeat after you.

3. Ask students to identify any words they don't know. Write any new words and phrases on the board and explain them. Some new phrases may include *sounds good, too hard, you can play too.* To teach the meanings of these terms, write the following dialogue on the board.

   Samir: It's *too* hot today.

   Binh: *Let's* go to the beach.

   Samir: *Sounds good.* Maybe my brother can come *too.*

   Explain that *too* sometimes means too much, and sometimes means *also.* Explain that *let's* is used to invite someone to do something and that *sounds good* means "I like what you say."

4. Play the tape or read the conversations at a natural rate. Have the students practice all the conversations and complete the last conversation. Then have pairs present the conversations to the class.

Page 17

Vocabulary Prompts

Refer to the general instructions on page xiv in the Introduction.

Presentation

To check comprehension, write the following sentences on the board and have volunteers come up and write in the correct vocabulary.

- The money you pay to take a class is a _____. (fee)
- When people do something like dance or sing and other people watch, it's called a _____. (performance)
- Pencils and paper are class _____. (supplies)
- All the players on the baseball team wear the same clothes. That's a _____. (uniform)
- Trees and birds are part of _____. (nature)
- When you learn how to do something, you learn the _____. (techniques)
- Drawing classes and judo classes are examples of _____ classes. (recreation)

Reading for Real

Refer to the general instructions on page xvii in the Introduction.

Preparation

1. To introduce the topic of the reading, write the phrase *take a class* on the board. Ask for student volunteers to explain the phrase. If no one can define it, give examples and your own definition. Ask questions such as the following:

   - What classes can you take in this city?
   - Can you take swimming lessons? Where?

2. Have students help you make a list of classes they know about in your community. Add and explain the classes listed in the reading, *folk dance, judo,* and *drawing.*

Exercise 2

Refer to the general instructions on page xvi in the Introduction.

Preparation

Point out that the information needed to answer the questions can be found in the reading.

Presentation

Have students complete the exercise with the same partners they had for the reading.

Answers to Exercise 2

1. a   2. c   3. c   4. d   5. a

Talk About It

Refer to the general instructions on page xvii in the Introduction.

Page 18

Vocabulary Prompts

Refer to the general instructions on page xiv in the Introduction.

Presentation

1. Give students this problem scenario. Define the word *stress*. Have students generating vocabulary and using their prior knowledge. Tell the following story or write it on the board:

   "I have a friend who has a lot of stress at her job. Can you help me think of some ideas to help my friend?"

2. Have students work in small groups to generate ideas. Write their ideas on the board. Encourage use of all the Vocabulary Prompts. What other vocabulary do they generate? Leave their ideas on the board.

Culture Corner

Refer to the general instructions on page xviii in the Introduction.

Presentation

1. Tell students they are going to read about job stress in the United States. Have students read the article individually.

2. Ask them to think about their own job situations. How do they compare with those people mentioned in the article?

3. If students in your class do not have jobs, ask them to think about their school or home life or have them think about a friend or family member who has a job.

Exercise 3

Refer to the general instructions on page xvi in the Introduction.

Presentation

1. Read through the directions with the students.

2. Emphasize that the answers they give will reflect how they feel and may not match other students' answers.

3. When students have finished answering the questions, have them read through the job-stress solutions and talk about them with a partner. Have them ask questions such as the following:

- Will those suggestions relieve job stress? Why or why not?
- Do you have a better idea?

Answers to Exercise 3

Answers will vary.

Exercise 4

Refer to the general instructions on page xvi in the Introduction.

Preparation

Before students complete the checklist, write the same list on the board under the title *Ways to Fight Stress.* Include students' suggestions from the Vocabulary Prompts activity.

Presentation

1. Ask the following questions:

- What does it mean to fight stress?
- What are some relaxing activities?
- What are some relaxation techniques? (walking, breathing slowly, listening to quiet music)
- What does it mean to exercise regularly?

2. After students have completed the exercise, survey the class to see which ways to fight stress are the most popular. Ask one or two volunteers to count the number of students in each category and write that number on the board next to the corresponding phrase.

Answers to Exercise 4

Answers will vary.

Page 19

Scene 2

Refer to the general instructions on page xviii in the Introduction.

Preparation

Introduce the topic of the lesson by asking students questions about their vacation activities. Ask questions such as the following:

- Do you like to go on vacation?
- Where do you like to go?
- What do you like to do there?

Presentation

Ask questions such as the following about Scene 2:

- Where is Chan going?
- What does he want to do?
- How long will he be there?
- How does Paul feel about Chan's schedule?

Extension

Have pairs of students role-play the Scene for the class in one of several ways. Bring in props or costumes to make the activity more interesting.

 Option 1: Students can perform the lines as written. You can assign pairs or let students choose their own partners.

Option 2: Students can make a simple substitution in some lines (by inserting their own weekend plans, for example).

Option 3: More advanced students can ad-lib a conversation on the topic treated in the Scene or imagine they are in the conversation with the characters in the Scene.

Sound Bites

Refer to the general instructions on pages xiii and xiv in the Introduction.

Preparation

Check students' prior knowledge of vocabulary such as *excited, hike, set up,* and *cool off.* Ask for definitions and examples. Clarify any words students are unsure of.

While You Listen

Presentation

1. Have students read the line under the Sound Bites heading.

2. Be sure students understand that the chart represents two days, with five activities on each day.

3. Tell students you will be playing the tape three times. The first time they should just listen for important information (such as times and activities). The second time they hear the tape, students should fill in the chart. For lower-level students, you may want to stop the tape after each day. The third time students hear the tape, they should check over their answers individually.

After You Listen

Preparation

1. Ask, "What else can Chan do on his trip?"

2. Write the students' suggestions on the board. Examples include the following: *read a book, play a guitar, listen to music on the radio,* and *take a nap.* This list will provide the language that students need to make a more relaxing schedule for Chan.

Presentation

1. On the board draw a chart similar to the Sound Bites chart. Have students copy it into their notebooks.

2. Have pairs of students create Chan's new schedule. Ask for volunteers to share theirs with the class.

Listening Script

Chan: I'm very excited about my trip to the mountains. On Saturday morning between 10:00 and 10:30, I want to set up camp near the trees. I plan to hike up the mountain at 10:30 and come back about 3:00 in the afternoon. I want to swim in the lake to cool off. I'll do that from 3:00 until 6:00 that afternoon.

I plan to wake up early Sunday morning at around 5:00. I want to go fishing in the lake from 6:00 in the morning to 2:00 in the afternoon. At 2:00 I plan to return home completely relaxed.

Answers to Sound Bites

Saturday Activity

set up camp 10:00–10:30

hike up mountain 10:30–3:00

swim in lake 3:00–6:00

Sunday Activity

wake up 5:00

go fishing 6:00–2:00

return home 2:00

Page 20

Spotlight on Verb + Infinitive

Refer to the general instructions on page xv in the Introduction.

Preparation

1. Ask students questions such as the following, using the infinitives in the unit:
   - What do you plan to do after school today?
   - Who plans to go to the park?
   - Who wants to play soccer?

2. Using the students' responses, write sentences on the board.
   - (José) plans to go to the park.
   - (Muon) wants to play soccer.

3. Underline the infinitives and explain that after some verbs, we use the word *to* and one more verb.

4. Elicit more student responses and write more sentences on the board. Ask a student to come up and underline the infinitives.

Exercise 5

Refer to the general instructions on page xvi in the Introduction.

Preparation

Review the list of infinitives used. Be sure students understand the meanings.

Presentation

1. Have students read the directions silently while you read them aloud.
2. Point out the different subjects in each sentence. Ask for volunteers to give examples of the correct forms.

Answers to Exercise 5

Answers will vary. Here are some possible answers:

1. I like to go to the beach.
2. My friends and I want to go dancing.
3. We also plan to see a play.
4. My girlfriend likes to play the guitar.
5. She likes to swim too.
6. Next weekend we plan to run in the park.

Person to Person

Refer to the general instructions on page xvi in the Introduction.

Presentation

1. Read the conversation and have students repeat the sentences after you. Play the tape if you wish.
2. Explain that students will practice the conversation once and then make changes to it. They will add any information about their own weekend plans that they can think of. The important thing is for them to talk about their plans using verbs and infinitives.
3. Have students work in pairs to practice the conversation and change it.
4. Have pairs of students read their new conversations to the class. To avoid intimidating students, who will be presenting their own ideas, try not to correct errors other than global errors (errors that affect comprehension).

Activity Masters

Activity Master 2-1 can be assigned any time after students have completed page 20.

Workbook

Workbook page 8 can be assigned after students have completed Student Book page 20.

Page 21

Spotlight on Adverbs of Frequency

Refer to the general instructions on page xv in the Introduction.

Preparation

1. To explain the concept of adverbs of frequency, quickly draw a calendar of the current month on the board or use an overhead transparency of one. Write *TV* on every Friday, Saturday, and Sunday. On the board write, "I always watch TV on the weekends." Write *read* on all but one or two of the weekend days. On the board, write, "I usually read books on the weekend." Continue to write in other activities, such as *music, movie, friends,* and *beach*. Write corresponding sentences about frequency.
2. Demonstrate the meaning of *never* by writing a negative sentence such as "I never work on the weekends." Point to the calendar to show that no work is listed.
3. To check comprehension about adverbs of frequency, ask questions such as the following:
   - How often do I watch TV on the weekends?
   - Do I usually read books on the weekends, or do I hardly ever read books?
4. To check comprehension, give additional examples and ask questions such as the following about them:
   - Marta watches TV every night. Does she hardly ever watch TV, or does she always watch TV?
   - Samir goes to a concert about once a year. Does he usually go to concerts or does he hardly ever go to concerts?
   - José plays soccer about five days every week. How often does he play soccer?
5. Explain that *rarely* and *seldom* can be used in place of *hardly ever*.

Presentation

Tell students to look at the bar chart and notice the percentages associated with each adverb. If students are unfamiliar with percentages, explain their use and model how to say them.

Exercise 6

Refer to the general instructions on page xvi in the Introduction.

Presentation

Emphasize that the word *ever* in the questions implies that students should think about their whole lives, and if they have done the activity even once, they should answer positively.

Answers to Exercise 6

Answers will vary. Here are some possible answers.

1. Yes, I always watch TV.
2. Yes, I sometimes go to the park.
3. Yes, I usually listen to music.
4. No, I hardly ever go dancing.

5. No, I never draw or paint.
6. Yes, I sometimes play guitar.
7. Yes, I often go to concerts.
8. No, I hardly ever go to museums.

In Your Experience

Refer to the general instructions on page xiv in the Introduction.

Workbook

Workbook pages 9 and 10 can be assigned after students have completed Student Book page 21.

Page 22

Vocabulary Prompts

Refer to the general instructions on page xiv in the Introduction.

Presentation

After students have discussed the Vocabulary Prompts in small groups, ask students questions such as the following:

- Which words do you know?
- I want to listen to music. Do I use a CD player or a camcorder?
- I want to make a movie of my daughter's birthday party. Do I use a CD player or camcorder?
- Which word is a general word for all the others?

Get Graphic

Refer to the general instructions on pages xviii and xix in the Introduction.

Preparation

Point out and explain the title of the bar graph.

- A product is something we make in factory. Is a car a product? What other products do you know?
- What is this graph about? Is it about how many electronic products are in homes or about how many are in schools?
- Is this information about 1992 or 1998?

Presentation

1. Have students read the directions and the graph individually.
2. Check comprehension about the graph by asking questions such as the following, or by having students help you create questions.
   - What percentage of homes have a TV?
   - What percentage of homes have a camcorder?
   - Do more homes have a VCR, or do more homes have a camcorder?
   - What electronic product is in the most homes? (Explain that *most* means the biggest percent or number, more than the others.)

Exercise 7

Refer to the general instructions on page xvi in the Introduction.

Presentation

1. Have students read the directions. To check comprehension, ask, "Where can we find the information we need to answer the questions?"
2. Point out to students that the first question asks for two products, so they will circle two letters.
3. Check to make sure that students are writing the percent sign correctly. For lower-level students, you may want to model it on the board.

Answers to Exercise 7

1. a   2. a. 98%   b. 88%   c. 52%   3. camcorder

In Your Experience

Refer to the general instructions on page xiv in the Introduction.

Presentation

1. Demonstrate how to make a bar graph. To gather the information, ask students to raise their hands as you ask who has the items in the bar graph on page 22. Ask questions such as the following:
   - How many students have a TV at home?
   - How many students have a radio at home?
2. Write a list on the board. Write the number of students next to each electronic product.
3. On the board quickly make a grid following the example in Get Graphic on page 22. Use numbers of students in place of the percentages of homes. Write the

names of the electronic products across the bottom. A grid for a class of 25 students will look like the following:

	TV	Radio	VCR	CD player	Camcorder
25					
20					
15					
10					
5					

4. Have a learner come to the board to plot the chart according to the information on the board. Fill in the bars to complete the graph.

Activity Masters

For further practice reading graphs, assign Activity Master 2-2.

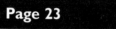
Page 23

Vocabulary Prompts

Refer to the general instructions on page xiv in the Introduction.

Issues and Answers

Refer to the general instructions on page xix in the Introduction.

Preparation

1. Introduce the topic of the lesson by asking students their opinions about TV. Ask questions such as the following:
   - Do you like to watch TV?
   - What's good about TV?
   - What's bad about TV?

2. Write one or two good and bad responses on the board. Write *pro* next to or above the "good" things about TV, and write *con* next to or above the bad things about TV.

Presentation

1. Ask students to give examples of important vocabulary, such as *boring, commercials,* and *news.* Explain any words they don't know.

2. Have students discuss the lists on page 23 and decide which statements they agree with and which ones they disagree with. Have volunteers share their opinions with the class.

Your Turn

Refer to the general instructions on page xiv in the Introduction.

Page 24

Wrap-Up

Refer to the general instructions on pages xix and xx in the Introduction.

Preparation

To prepare students for Wrap-Up, ask questions about the fun things they do. Explain that an *idea* is what you think.

Extension

Have students write sentences from the information in the T-charts. Write a couple of example sentences on the board, such as, "I like to walk in the park and play soccer. My partner likes to read books and watch TV."

Think About Learning

Refer to the general instructions on pages xix and xx in the Introduction.

Workbook

Workbook pages 11 and 12 can be assigned after students have completed Student Book page 24.

ANSWERS TO PROGRESS CHECKS
Progress Check A
Speak or Write

1. Paul and Chan are talking about Chan's trip.
2. Chan is going to the mountains to go camping.
3. Paul is surprised because Chan is doing so much during his trip. Chan's trip is two days.
4. Answers will vary.

Listening Script

Answers are underlined.

Paul and Chan are friends. They (1) <u>like to</u> relax on the weekends. They (2) <u>want to</u> go camping. They (3) <u>plan to</u> go camping in the mountains next Saturday. They (4) <u>have</u> a problem. Chan (5) <u>wants to</u> swim and go fishing. Paul (6) <u>doesn't like</u> the lake. He (7) <u>plans to</u> hike and read all weekend.

Progress Check B
Language Structures

1. Maria <u>likes</u> to swim.
2. Samir and José <u>don't like</u> to swim.
3. Antonio usually <u>works</u> on Saturdays.
4. José and Ana <u>work</u> hard.
5. Lin <u>doesn't like</u> loud music.
6. Ling and Ly <u>don't have</u> jobs.

Content

1. d   2. a   3. b   4. c

ANSWERS TO ACTIVITY MASTERS
Activity Master 2-1

Answers will vary.

Activity Master 2-2

1. F   2. T   3. F   4. T   5. F   6. T   7. F   8. T

UNIT 2

WORKBOOK ANSWERS

Practice 1

Story 1

1. work   2. don't work   3. do   4. plays

5. listens   6. see   7. don't come   8. visit

Story 2

1. likes   2. doesn't like   3. loves

4. doesn't like   5. like   6. visit

Practice 2

Conversation 1

1. want to do   2. plan to go   3. like to listen

4. plan to eat   5. want to have

Conversation 2

1. plans to camp   2. wants to put   3. wants to hike   4. plans to swim

Practice 3

1. always   2. never   3. often   4. hardly ever

Practice 4

1. People in the United States usually like to relax on weekends.

2. People in the United States sometimes visit friends or family.

3. Children usually play sports outside in hot or cold weather.

4. Teenagers often like to go shopping with their friends.

5. Families sometimes like to eat at restaurants on the weekends.

Practice 5

1. Jessica usually plays the piano.

2. She always does homework. She always plays soccer.

3. She sometimes talks on the phone.

4. She hardly ever reads.

5. Answers will vary. Here are some possible answers:
   She never goes to work. She never plays baseball.

REPRODUCIBLE MASTER
UNIT 2

PROGRESS CHECK A

SPEAK OR WRITE

Look at the pictures from Unit 2. Use the questions below to talk or
write about each picture.

Questions

1. What are Paul and Chan talking about in these pictures?

2. Where is Chan going?

3. How does Paul feel in the second picture? Why?

4. What do you like to do on weekends?

LISTEN

Listen and write the missing words.

Paul and Chan are friends. They (1) _____ relax on the weekends.

They (2) _____ go camping. They (3) _____ go camping in

the mountains next Saturday. They (4) _____ a problem.

Chan (5) _____ swim and go fishing. Paul (6) _____ the lake.

He _____ (7) hike and read all weekend.

REPRODUCIBLE MASTER
UNIT 2

PROGRESS CHECK B

LANGUAGE STRUCTURES

Write the verbs. Use the simple present.

1. Maria (*like*) _____ to swim.

2. Samir and José (*not/like*) _____ to swim.

3. Antonio usually (*work*) _____ on Saturdays.

4. José and Ana (*work*) _____ hard.

5. Lin (*not/like*) _____ loud music.

6. Ling and Ly (*not/have*) _____ jobs.

CONTENT

Match the words on the right with the sentences on the left. Write the correct letter in the blank.

1. Money for a class is a _____.   a. stress

2. David is nervous and angry at work. He   b. schedule
   has job _____.

                                                 c. relax

3. Maria plans to clean the house at 10:00, go
   shopping at 2:00, and cook dinner at 5:00.   d. fee
   She has a busy _____.

4. I come home from work. I sit down, listen
   to music, and close my eyes. I _____.

Name _____ Date _____

What do you plan to do this weekend?

Mario and Lin are talking about the weekend. Practice this conversation with a partner.

Mario: What do you plan to do this weekend, Lin?

Lin: I plan to go dancing.

Mario: When?

Lin: Saturday night. It's my friend's birthday.

Mario: Sounds good.

Talk to five classmates. Practice this conversation and write the answers in the chart below.

Student A: What do you plan to do this weekend?

Student B: I plan to _____.

Student A: When?

Student B: _____.

Name	What	When

REPRODUCIBLE MASTER
UNIT 2

ACTIVITY MASTER 2-2

MORE GRAPHIC SKILLS

This bar graph tells about the activities the students at Westside Adult Center like to do on weekends. Study the graph and read the sentences below. Put a check under *true* or *false*.

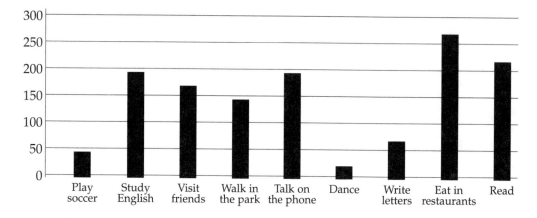

	True	False
1. One hundred twenty-five students like to eat in restaurants.	_____	_____
2. More students like to play soccer than dance.	_____	_____
3. All the students like to read.	_____	_____
4. More than one hundred twenty-five students like to talk on the telephone.	_____	_____
5. Two hundred fifty students like to study English on the weekends.	_____	_____
6. More students like to talk on the telephone than write letters.	_____	_____
7. Only twenty-five students like to play soccer.	_____	_____
8. More students like to visit their friends than write letters.	_____	_____

Unit 3 Problem Solving in the Neighborhood

OVERVIEW

Objectives

Skills and Structures

Listen to safety ideas

Speak about neighborhood life

Solve a public problem

Learn about a job as a guard

Read and write a report

Use *there is/there are/there was/there were*

Use simple past of regular and irregular verbs

Use prepositions of location

Complete a T-chart

SCANS Competencies

Solve problems: Student Book, Scene 1, page 25; Student Book, Sound Bites, page 26; Student Book, Reading for Real, page 29, Student Book, Issues and Answers, page 35; Workbook, Read, Think, and Write, page 17; Teacher's Manual, Reading for Real, page 51.

Teach others: Student Book, Scene 2, page 31; Teacher's Manual, Activity Master 3-2.

Realia

Crime Stoppers flyer, Neighborhood Watch flyer, a neighborhood newsletter

A police report form, an incident form from your school's security officer

Letter-sized file folders—as many as half the number of students present—to be used as dividers for an information-gap activity.

A water utility bill

Newspaper job ads for a security guard

ACTIVITY NOTES

Page 25

Scene 1

Preparation

1. Write *neighborhood* on the board. Draw some houses and apartments. Put a circle around them. Point to the word and the drawing and say the word *neighborhood*.

2. Write the word *neighbors* and make some stick figures next to the homes. Point to the stick figures and say, "Hi, neighbor!"

3. Talk about the neighborhood around the school to help learners visualize a real neighborhood. Ask students for information, and on the board either draw or write the school, streets, stores, and other things that students mention.

4. Weave some of the new vocabulary into the introductory activity and also encourage students to come up with as many of these words as they can:

   - park, trees, police station, street lights, hospital, pay phone, bus stop, bus station, playground, cars, traffic
   - restaurant, supermarket, library, bank, check cashing store, department store, movie theater, swimming pool, garage, fence, trash, next-door neighbor

Presentation

1. Ask questions such as the following about the pictures in Scene 1:
   - How do the people in the first picture know each other?
   - Do you think they are friends? Why or why not?
   - Who brought the ladder? How does he know these people?
   - How does the girl feel in the third picture?

Extension

Have pairs of students role-play the Scene in one of several ways. Bring in props or costumes to make the activity more interesting.

Option 1: Students can perform the lines as written. You can assign pairs or let students choose their own partners.

Option 2: Students can make a simple substitution in some lines (by inserting a different neighborhood problem for example).

Option 3: More advanced students can ad-lib a conversation on the topic treated in the Scene or imagine they are in the conversation with the characters in the Scene.

Page 26

Vocabulary Prompts

Presentation

1. Display flyers or newsletters about Crime Stoppers or Neighborhood Watch. Also, display a police report form, or get an incident form from the school administrator or security officer in charge of school safety. Pass these papers around for students to skim and pass on.

2. To check comprehension of Vocabulary Prompts, ask students if they know which papers are to help people *report* problems. Ask which papers are to help people *solve* problems.

3. Also, ask if students know which papers are to help people *prevent* problems, or stop problems before they start. Ask students if they have experience trying to prevent, solve, or report a problem.

Sound Bites

Preparation

1. Review the words *safe* and *dangerous.* Have students define them and give examples to the class. Write their examples on the board under the headings *Safe* and *Dangerous.*

2. Focus students' attention on personal safety by asking questions such as the following:
   - Do you feel safe in your neighborhood during the day?
   - Do you feel safe walking at night?
   - Is it dangerous to walk alone there at night?
   - Do you feel safer in your native country or in the United States?

Before You Listen

Presentation

After students have reviewed the pictures, discuss each picture with the class to make sure everyone understands what the pictures show. Ask questions such as these.

- Does the first picture show one or two neighborhoods? Does it look like a nice area? Why?
- In the second picture is the woman in the apartment happy or unhappy? Why do you think she feels that way?

While You Listen

Presentation

1. Tell students that they will hear three conversations. Explain that you will play the tape three times and that they should try to listen for the specific information asked for in the questions. Tell them that they do not have to write anything the first time they listen; they will write their answers when you play the tape the second time. When you play the tape the third time, they will check their answers.

2. Play the tape three times. When you play the tape the second time, students should mark their answers in their books. When you play the tape the third time, students should check their answers individually.

After You Listen

Presentation

After students have reviewed their answers with a partner or a small group, review any questions that have produced more than one answer.

Listening Script

1. Maria: Samira, how is your new neighborhood?

   Samira: It's great, Maria. There are big trees and bright lights. I feel safe in this neighborhood.

   Maria: How nice! Can I come see it soon?

2. Operator: Hello. Crime Stoppers Office.

   Neighbor: Yes, I want to report something bad happening in my neighborhood.

   Operator: What is it?

   Neighbor: Well, I don't want to tell you my name.

Operator:	No problem. We give your report a number only, no names. What do you want to report?
Neighbor:	There are many cars in front of my neighbor's apartment day and night. People get out of the cars. They go into that apartment and come out in 5 or 10 minutes. I think maybe they buy drugs there.
Operator:	What's the address?
Neighbor:	6739 Victoria Street.
Operator:	Thank you. Your report number is 24781. Call back if you can.

3.
David:	Kathy, there is a Neighborhood Watch meeting tonight. Do you and your husband want to come?
Kathy:	Sure. What exactly is a Neighborhood Watch meeting, David?
David:	A Neighborhood Watch meeting is for neighbors. We meet in my apartment and talk about neighborhood problems.
Kathy:	Do you pay money?
David:	No, we try to fix problems in the neighborhood. Do you want to come?
Kathy:	Yes! There's trash on our street. Maybe we can clean it.

Answers to Sound Bites

1. Yes, there are. She feels safe.

2. There may be people buying drugs at the neighbor's apartment. The officer doesn't ask for the caller's name.

3. Neighbors get together to talk about problems in the neighborhood. Kathy wants to clean up the trash on the street.

In Your Experience

Presentation

1. Have students refer to the lists on the board to help them write sentences describing their neighborhoods.

2. Write these sentence starters on the board to encourage students to write complete sentences and to introduce the structure focus of the next Spotlight Box:

   • My neighborhood has good points. There is/are _____.

   • My neighborhood has some bad points too. There is/are _____.

3. As students read sentences to the class, make a mental note of errors in structure to be addressed after the next Spotlight Box activities.

Page 27

Spotlight on *There Is, There Are, There Was, There Were*

Preparation

1. Have students volunteer to write some of their sentences on the board from the previous In Your Experience activity.

2. Underline *There is,* and *There are* in the sentences. Circle structure errors, but don't correct them. Explain that the sentences will be reviewed and corrected after the class studies the next Spotlight Box.

Presentation

1. Have students read through the sentences in the Spotlight Box. Point out that there are four structures presented. Elicit the present-tense forms of the verb *be,* which the students already know.
2. To check comprehension, ask pairs of students to make the singular sentences plural and vice versa.
3. In addition to the structures listed on the board, add *There is no, There are no, There was no, There were no.* These structures are also used in the unit.

Extension

Review and correct the sentences on the board with the class. Add more student sentences and ask volunteers to check and correct errors. Also practice question formation. Change a sentence on the board into a question. Ask for volunteers to change the other sentences into questions.

Exercise 1

Presentation

Ask students to read through the list of words and give examples of each. Define any words the students do not understand.

Answers to Exercise 1

1. trees   2. lights   3. playground   4. trash   5. neighborhood

In Your Experience

Preparation

Give students five minutes to brainstorm anything they can remember about their previous neighborhood and to write it in their notebooks. Remind them that they do not have to write sentences.

Activity Masters

Activity Master 3-1 can be assigned after students have completed page 27.

Presentation

To model this activity, choose a student to interview and write his or her name in the first box next to *Name.* Then ask the questions and write *yes* or *no* in the boxes as the student answers your questions. Choose another student to interview. Have students practice reading the interview questions as you write a student's responses in the boxes. Then pass out the papers and read the instructions to the students.

Workbook

Workbook pages 13 and 14 can be assigned after students have completed Student Book page 27.

Person to Person

Preparation

1. Pre-teach this vocabulary if needed: *noises, back stairs*, and *traffic*.

2. Have students look at the pictures above each conversation. Elicit what they think the conversation is about.

3. In the first conversation ask for volunteers to explain what 911 is. If no one can explain it, tell students that it is a telephone number for calling the police, ambulance service, or fire department and that it should be used in extreme emergencies only.

Extension

1. Write on the board a list of possible examples of crime: *fight, assault, robbery, home burglary, car burglary, car theft, hit-and-run accident, purse-snatching*.

2. Have students define the crime list, either by giving an example or by acting out the situation for you and others to define.

3. Use the examples of crime to model *There is/There are/There was/There were* sentences. For example, say, "There were two robberies at that store." Have students tell their own sentences to a partner.

Activity Masters

Activity Master 3-2 can be assigned after students have completed page 28.

Preparation

1. Copy a class set of handouts and then cut off the bottom two sets of answer keys, A Answers and B Answers.

2. Use page 6, Culture Corner, Unit 1, to review clarification techniques.

3. Elicit any prior knowledge of the following vocabulary: *safety tips, friend, alone, yell, self-defense, lock, ID*, and *blinds*. Clarify any words students are unfamiliar with.

Presentation

Learners will need 25 to 40 minutes to complete this jigsaw reading activity.

1. Tell students they are going to read and teach each other some safety tips.

2. Put students in pairs. Have them decide who is Student A and who is Student B. (Check by asking, "Who is A? Who is B?")

3. Distribute papers with answer keys cut off.

4. Group Student As together and give them the A answers. Group Student Bs together and give them the B answers. Have students complete and review their tips in these groups. Circulate to assist with comprehension and pronunciation. (This part of the activity will take 10 to 15 minutes.)

5. Have students return to their partners and share tips. One student should read as the other student writes the tip. Partners must help each other understand each tip. Circulate to check that students are not just copying answers from each other. You may want to put a letter-sized file folder between Student A and Student B to encourage oral communication and discourage copying. (This part of the activity will take about 15 minutes.)

6. Review tips with the whole class. Ask students if they like teaching each other these tips. Ask students if it is more difficult to listen and write or to speak and explain.

Extension

Ask the class to add more tips to the list. For example, "Don't hide a house key outside."

Reading for Real

Preparation

1. Point to the building, the bucket, and the metal object. Say, "You're going to read about a very tall, 14-story water tank made out of steel that some people say is really ugly."
2. Have the class look at the photo of the water tank, and ask learners if they think the water tank is attractive or ugly.

Presentation

1. Give students enough time to read each paragraph silently (about five minutes). At the end of each paragraph, ask comprehension questions such as the following:

   - Paragraph 1: How big is the water tank? How many gallons of water does it hold? What is it made out of?
   - Paragraph 2: What is the problem? What do some people want to do?
   - Paragraph 3: There was a meeting about the tank. What did the people decide to do?

Exercise 2

Presentation

1. Remind students to look for the answers in the reading.
2. With the class discuss the students' answers to question 4.

Answers to Exercise 2

1. It's 14 stories tall.
2. Some people think the tank is very ugly.
3. It costs $430,000.
4. Answers will vary.

Your Turn

Presentation

1. Have students work in groups of four or five. Each group should assign a secretary to write down the group's ideas before starting to work. Check to make sure groups have done this by asking the group secretaries to raise their hands.
2. Give students a time limit of approximately 15 minutes for this exercise. Tell them to think of things they would like to change as well as what they could do to change them.

Vocabulary Prompts

Presentation

To check comprehension, write the following sentences on the board and have volunteers come up and write in the correct Vocabulary Prompt.

People ask you questions about yourself at an _____. (interview)

To watch something so that nothing bad happens is to _____ it. (protect)

Something I own is my _____. (property)

Telling someone what I think she should do is _____. (advice)

When I write about things that happened, I write a _____. (report)

Culture Corner

Preparation

Write these words on the board: *condominium, kids, vandalism, graffiti.* Draw a broken window on the board. Draw a wall with some words scrawled on it. Tell a story about a security guard, some children, and the broken window. Use the words *vandalism* and *graffiti.* For example, say, "The kids were putting graffiti on the walls, writing their nicknames with spray paint. The security guard saw a kid pick up a rock and throw it through a window. This was vandalism, not an accident."

Presentation

1. Ask for volunteers to read the directions and the introductory paragraph aloud to the class.

2. If students have never seen an interview format before, point out that colons are used instead of quotation marks, and that when the speaker changes, a new line is always started.

3. Have students work in pairs to read the dialogue to each other. If needed, model this procedure with a volunteer before students proceed.

Scene 2

Preparation

1. On the board write the words *renter* and *home owner.* Ask for volunteers to explain similarities and differences. If students have trouble, list some of the major differences on the board.

2. Focus students' attention on their own situations by asking questions such as the following:

   • Are you a renter or a home owner?

   • Is it easy or difficult to buy a home? Why?

Presentation

Ask questions about Scene 2. Here are some examples:

   • Why did Cha-Soon and Yung bring Margarita a present?

   • How does Margarita feel about her present in the second picture?

   • What does Cha-Soon tell her that makes her change her mind?

Extension

Option 1: Students can perform the lines as written. You can assign pairs or let students choose their own partners.

Option 2: Students can make a simple substitution in some lines (by inserting a custom from their native country, for example).

Option 3: More advanced students can ad-lib a conversation on the topic treated in the Scene or imagine they are in the conversation with the characters in the Scene.

Vocabulary Prompts

Presentation

To check comprehension, write the following story on the board. Have students work in pairs to fill in the blanks with the correct words.

My brother finally _____ (bought) a house last week. He _____ (paid) a lot of money for it, but he had _____ (saved) money for two years before he found it, so he had a very large _____ (downpayment). Because of that, he can afford his _____ every month. (mortgage)

Sound Bites

Before You Listen

Preparation

List ways to get money for a new house as a whole-class activity after students have worked in small groups but before they have listened to the tape. This will prepare students for While You Listen and After You Listen.

1. Tell students that they will hear a conversation between Margarita and Cha-Soon. Explain that you will play the tape three times and that they should try to listen for the specific information asked for in the questions. Tell them that they do not have to write anything the first time they listen; they will write their answers when you play the tape the second time. When you play the tape the third time, they will check their answers.

2. Play the tape three times. When you play the tape the second time, students should mark their answers. When you play the tape the third time, students should check their answers individually.

After You Listen

Presentation

1. After students have checked their answers with a partner or a small group, review any questions that have produced more than one answer.

2. Play the tape of the conversations or read them to the class.

Listening Script

Cha-Soon:	Margarita, your new house is wonderful!
Margarita:	Thank you! I really like it. My sister, my uncle, and I bought it together.
Cha-Soon:	Did you save money for a long time?

Margarita:	Yes, we lived together in a small apartment. We all had two jobs, so we saved a lot of extra money.
Cha-Soon:	How much of a down payment did you need?
Margarita:	We paid $24,000 as a down payment.
Cha-Soon:	So how many years will you pay the mortgage?
Margarita:	Thirty years.
Cha-Soon:	I hope you like the neighborhood!
Margarita:	Don't worry! I love this neighborhood.

Answers to Sound Bites

Ways to get money for a new house:

buy together with other family members

share expenses

rent a small apartment

have two jobs

make sure that everybody works

don't spend extra money

save extra money

Page 32

Spotlight on Simple Past of Regular and Irregular Verbs

Preparation

Review the simple past by using the past tense as you go over the list from Scene 2. Point to the list and say, "What did Margarita do to get money for a new house? She bought it with other family members," and so on.

Presentation

Model the various pronunciations of *-ed* in the regular simple past forms in the Spotlight Box. Have students repeat them after you.

Exercise 3

Presentation

1. Ask students to read over the paragraph. Clarify any words they do not understand, including *for sale* and *loan*.
2. Have students work individually to fill in the paragraph. Remind them that all the verbs they need are in the Spotlight Box.
3. Review the answers with the class. Call on volunteers to read the paragraph aloud.

Answers to Exercise 3

| 1. went | 2. talked | 3. said | 4. bought |
| 5. found | 6. took | 7. asked | |

Person to Person

Presentation

1. Read the conversations and have students repeat the sentences after you.

2. Explain that students will practice the conversation once and then make changes to it. They will add any information about their own situations that they can think of. The important thing is for them to talk about an event or situation in the past.

3. Have students work in pairs to practice the conversation and change it.

4. Have pairs of students read their new conversations to the class. To avoid intimidating students, who will be presenting their own ideas, try not to correct errors other than global errors (errors that affect comprehension).

Workbook

Workbook page 15 can be assigned after students have completed Student Book page 32.

Page 33

Spotlight on Prepositions of Location

Preparation

Introduce the prepositions with a Total Physical Response (TPR) activity: students listen and follow commands without speaking. Use the prepositions in the book. Ask students to listen and do what you say. Check to see who responds correctly before performing the action yourself. Use commands such as the following:

- Stand *beside* your chair.
- Put your pencil *inside* your notebook.
- Put your hand *between* your ESL notebook and your Student Book.
- Hold your book *behind* your chair.

Presentation

Tell students to study the art in the Spotlight Box. Elicit the fact that the prepositions refer to where the kitten is in *relation* to something else (the house, the feet, the trash bag, etc.).

Answers to Exercise 4

1. between   2. outside   3. behind   4. beside   5. inside

Workbook

Workbook page 16 can be assigned after students have completed Student Book page 33.

Page 34

Get Graphic

Presentation

1. Ask students why there are three columns on the chart. How would this help the guard if there were a problem?

2. Use locations at your school as a model to review Vocabulary Prompts and to explain some locations on the graph.

Extension

Invite the school's security officer to visit your class. Ask the officer some questions similar to those in the Culture Corner reading on page 30 about his or her job.

Exercise 5

Presentation

Point out that students will find all the answers in the checklist. When students have finished reviewing their partner's answers, discuss any discrepancies with the class.

Answers to Exercise 5

1. three times   2. The lights were out. The checklist says so.

3. parking lot, front door, rear door, swimming pool

Page 35

Issues and Answers

Preparation

Ask students if they know a security guard. In front of the class, interview students who do. Ask questions such as the following:

- Is this person from your home country?
- When did this person come to the United States?
- Does this person go to school to study English?
- How did this person find the job?

Extension

Show students a newspaper ad for a security guard. Write the job requirements on the board. Compare them to what students already know about the job.

Page 36

Wrap-Up

Extension

1. Collect the students' sentences on the advantages and disadvantages of being a security guard.

2. Put a sign on one wall with the word *advantages* and on the opposite wall, one with the word *disadvantages*. (Put up additional signs on other walls alternating *advantages* and *disadvantages* to create more choices for students.)

3. Read one sentence and have students go to the appropriate wall, depending on whether they consider it an advantage or disadvantage. Have students share reasons with the group at their wall and then with the whole class.

4. Read another sentence. Students should make a decision and move to the wall of their choice. Continue with discussion and more sentences.

5. Include some sentences that could go either way—for example, "They work in the afternoon." (In Culture Corner, Cass likes to work in the afternoon so he can take care of his daughter in the morning. For him, it is an advantage.)

Workbook

Workbook pages 17 and 18 can be assigned after students have completed Student Book page 36.

ANSWERS TO PROGRESS CHECKS

Progress Check A

Speak or Write

Answers will vary. Here are some possible answers.

1. She gives her soap.

2. She is surprised.

3. She says it's for good luck.

4. She's happy.

Listening Script

(Answers are underlined.)

Marta (1) is tired today. Last night there (2) was a problem in her neighborhood. At 11:00 P.M. Marta (3) saw a man (4) outside her neighbor's house. He broke a window and went (5) inside. Marta (6) called the police. A policeman (7) went to the neighbor's house. He (8) found the man. Then he (9) talked to Marta. He (10) asked questions and (11) wrote a report. Marta didn't go to sleep until 2:00 A.M. That's why Marta is tired today.

Progress Check B

Language Structures

1. are *or* aren't
2. were *or* weren't
3. is
4. isn't
5. are
6. was *or* wasn't, wasn't
7. was
8. was

Content

1. True   2. False   3. True   4. False

ANSWERS TO ACTIVITY MASTERS

Activity Master 3-1

Answers will vary.

Activity Master 3-2

A
Answers:
1. friend   2. night   3. Look around   4. where, how long   5. pay phones

B
Answers:
1. windows   2. door   3. ID   4. no   5. close

Answers also appear at the bottom of the master.

UNIT 3

WORKBOOK ANSWERS

Practice 1

1. Is, isn't   2. is, is   3. Are, aren't

Practice 3

1. library   2. department store   3. bank

Practice 4

1. took   2. wrote   3. found   4. said   5. got

6. paid   7. found   8. wrote   9. got   10. got

Practice 5

1. beside (or next to)   2. behind

3. between   4. on the corner of

REPRODUCIBLE MASTER
UNIT 3

PROGRESS CHECK A

SPEAK OR WRITE

Look at the pictures from Unit 3. Use the questions below to speak
or write about the pictures.

Questions

1. What does Yung give Margarita?

2. How does Margarita feel about the gift at first?

3. What does Yung explain about the meaning of the gift?

4. How does Margarita feel after Yung explains the meaning of
   the gift?

LISTEN

Listen and write the missing words. Use the words below.

is	wrote	went	found	asked
inside	outside	called	talked	saw	was

Marta (1) _____ tired today. Last night there (2) _____ a problem in her

neighborhood. At 11:00 P.M. Marta (3) _____ a man (4) _____ her neighbor's

house. He broke a window and went (5) _____. Marta (6) _____ the police.

A policeman (7) _____ to the neighbor's house. He (8) _____ the man. Then

he (9) _____ to Marta. He (10) _____ questions and (11) _____ a report.

Marta didn't go to sleep until 2:00 A.M. That's why Marta is tired today.

Name _____ Date _____

PROGRESS CHECK B

LANGUAGE STRUCTURES

Write the missing words. Use the present or past of *be*.

1. There _____ many trees in my neighborhood.

2. There _____ many trees in my old neighborhood
   in my country.

3. There _____ one teacher in this class.

4. Is there a bus station next to the library?

   No, there _____.

5. There _____ many cars in the United States.

6. _____ there a cat in the tree an hour ago?

   No, there _____.

7. Were there many students in class yesterday?

   Yes, there _____.

8. There _____ an accident on Elm Street yesterday.

CONTENT

Read the sentences. Circle *T* for *true* and *F* for *false*.

1. T F   Security guards protect property.

2. T F   Neighborhood Watch is the name of a TV program.

3. T F   In a good neighborhood, neighbors sometimes work
          together to take care of problems.

4. T F   Security guards are police officers.

Name _____ Date _____

YOUR NEIGHBORHOOD

Walk around the classroom. Ask questions about three of your classmates' neighborhoods now (in the United States) and before (in their native countries). Write *yes* or *no* in the boxes.

Ask these questions.

1. Are there many trees in your neighborhood now?
   Were there many trees in your neighborhood before?

2. Are there many cars in your neighborhood now?
   Were there many cars in your neighborhood before?

3. Are there street lights in your neighborhood now?
   Were there street lights in your neighborhood before?

4. Is there a police station in your neighborhood now?
   Was there a police station in your neighborhood before?

Name	1.		2.		3.	
	now	**before**	**now**	**before**	**now**	**before**
1. many trees						
2. many cars						
3. street lights						
4. a police station						

REPRODUCIBLE MASTER
UNIT 3   ACTIVITY MASTER 3-2

MORE READING FOR REAL

Safety Tips In the Neighborhood — Part A

Note: See Teacher's Manual page 50 for complete directions on this activity.

1. Walk with a _____.

2. Be careful at _____. Stay in the light.

3. _____ _____ when you are alone.

4. When alone, tell a friend _____ and

_____ _____ you will be out.

5. Know the location of _____

_____. Calls to 911 are free.

Safety Tips At Home — Part B

1. Lock all your doors and _____ day and night.

2. Know who is at the _____ before you open it.

3. Ask to see _____ from a person you don't know.

4. If the person asks to use the phone, say _____.

   You can call the number for the person.

5. _____ the blinds at night.

✂ -

A Answers: 1. friend   2. night   3. Look around
4. where, how long   5. pay phones

✂ -

B Answers: 1. windows   2. door   3. ID   4. no   5. Close

UNIT 4

OVERVIEW

Objectives

Skills and Structures

Talk about group work

Learn about successful Americans

Read a work history

Understand a time line

Read about the qualities of a leader

Use regular simple past

Use simple past in yes/no questions and negative statements

Use past time expressions

SCANS Competencies

Exercise leadership: Student Book, Culture Corner, page 42; Student Book, Issues and Answers, page 47; Teacher's Manual, Activity Master 4-1.

Monitor and correct performance: Student Book, Spotlight on Simple Past in Affirmative Statements, pronunciation practice, page 39; Student Book, Scene 2, page 43; Student Book, Sound Bites, After You Listen, page 43; Teacher's Manual, Activity Master 4-2.

Participate as a member of a team: Student Book, Culture Corner, page 42; Student Book, Get Graphic, Your Turn, page 46; Teacher's Manual, Activity Master 4-1.

Realia

Penny or five-dollar bill

Newspaper or magazine photo of the President of the United States or another famous person

World map

U.S. map

Current-year calendar

Newsprint paper; markers or crayons

ACTIVITY NOTES

Page 37

Scene 1

Preparation

1. Write *Successful* on the board. Discuss the meaning of this word. Note that the second page of the unit gives this definition: *To be successful means to do something well.*

2. Practice using the word *successful*. Have students define *successful student, successful business,* the title *Successful Americans,* and so on.

3. Pull out a penny or a five-dollar bill. Ask whose picture is on it. Tell a brief story about Lincoln. Say, "Abraham Lincoln was born in 1809 into a poor family. He had many problems in his life, but he always worked hard. He became President of the United States in 1861. It was a difficult time. There was a civil war between Northern and Southern states, but Lincoln worked to keep the country together. And he did! He is now remembered as one of the great United States Presidents." Tell students they will read and hear more success stories in this unit.

4. Before students work independently on Scene 1, introduce or review key concepts related to team work.

5. Review the meaning of *group work*—students working together. Working as a member of a team is a key SCANS competency that can be developed in the classroom. If assignment of roles in a group is a new concept for the class, use the roles and duties in this unit to introduce the concept.

6. Write the following on the board: *leader, secretary, reporter, time keeper*. In a separate list write the following: *watches the clock, reports, organizes and keeps the group working, writes the answers*.

7. Explain that sometimes each person in a group has a different job. Ask students to look at the board and to match the job duty with the name of that job. For example, say, "Who do you think watches the clock? What's the name of that job?" Continue until you have asked questions about all four jobs.

Presentation

After students have reviewed the pictures and answered the questions, explain that this kind of class work is common in the United States. Ask students whether they have worked in teams before, either at their job or in a classroom in their native countries. Was the group successful? Why or why not?

Extension

Have pairs of students role-play the Scene in one of several ways. Bring in props or costumes to make the activity more interesting.

Option 1: Students can perform the lines as written. You can assign pairs or let students choose their own partners.

Option 2: Students can make a simple substitution in some lines (by inserting a different class project for example).

Option 3: More advanced students can ad-lib a conversation on the topic treated in the Scene or imagine they are in the conversation with the characters in the Scene.

Page 38

Sound Bites

Before You Listen

Preparation

1. If students do not already know it, define and give examples of *immigrant*—a person from one country coming into a new country to make a home there.

2. Check the location of the countries on a world map. Practice pronunciation of the countries.

3. Ask students to predict what the people do using the pictures on the chart.

While You Listen

Preparation

Write on the board the words *date moved to the United States* followed by a blank line. Say, "Sally was born in Canada in 1960. She moved to the United States in 1975. She got married in 1978." Have a student write the correct date (1975) on the line. Give other examples until a majority of students can isolate the correct date.

Presentation

1. Tell students that they will hear about six people. Explain that you will play a tape three times and that they should try to listen for the specific information in the chart. Tell them that they do not have to write anything the first time they listen; they will write their answers when you play the tape the second time. Remind them that the names of the countries referred to in the tape are listed above the chart. When you play the tape the third time, they will check their answers.

2. Play the tape three times. When you play the tape the second time, students should mark their answers in their books. When you play the tape the third time, students should check their answers individually.

After You Listen

Presentation

After students have checked their answers with a partner, go over the correct answers with the class. Pay special attention to the years listed. You may want to play the tape a fourth time for sections that students found difficult.

Listening Script

1. Our group learned about Martina Navratilova. She started to play tennis when she was a young girl in Czechoslovakia. In 1975 she moved to the United States. Martina became the world's top female tennis player.

2. An Wang moved to the United States from China in 1945. He was a computer engineer and a business man. He started a computer company, Wang Laboratories. It became a successful company. An Wang died in 1990.

3. We read about Alexander Graham Bell. He invented the telephone. Many people forget that he did not come from this country. He was born in Scotland and moved to the United States in 1871. We hear his name today in the names of many Bell telephone companies in the United States.

4. Roberto Clemente played baseball very well. He was born in Puerto Rico, and he moved to the United States in 1955. He won the Most Valuable Player award two times. He liked to help people too. He wanted to help the people in Nicaragua after a bad earthquake. He took food and medicine in a plane, but the plane crashed, and he died. Roberto Clemente was a good man and a good baseball player.

5. Our group learned about Gloria Estefan. She was born in Cuba and moved to the United States in 1959. She is a famous singer. Gloria was in a bad bus accident when she was 32 years old. She broke her back, and she was in the hospital a long time. She worked hard to get better. Now she can sing, walk, and dance better than most people!

6. In 1997 Madeleine Albright became the first woman Secretary of State for the United States. She was born in Czechoslovakia, and she lived in many countries. She moved to the United States in 1948. She speaks five languages: English, French, Czech, Russian, and Polish.

Answers to Sound Bites

1. Czechoslovakia, 1975   2. China, 1945   3. Scotland, 1871
4. Puerto Rico, 1955   5. Cuba, 1959   6. Czechoslovakia, 1948

Your Turn

Extension

Have students introduce themselves to each other in groups of four, using the same format as the Sound Bites information.

- I am _____.
- I am from _____.
- I moved to the United States in _____.

Page 39

Spotlight on Simple Past in Affirmative Statements

Preparation

1. Write *work, worked* on the board. Use *work* and *worked* in two sentences about your work history. For example, "I worked in a junior high school from 1984 to 1987. Now I work at City Center Adult School."

2. Ask which word is used to talk about the past. Assess how many students already recognize *-ed* as showing past action.

3. Review the meaning of the words *consonant* and *vowel* before introducing the spelling guidelines.

4. Practice the three variations in pronunciation of *ed* orally before reading the pronunciation rules. Say, "worked, started, moved." Have students listen to and identify the ending sounds.

Exercise 1

Preparation

1. If needed, define *move* and *invent*.

2. Before doing the written exercises, have students predict and practice the pronunciation of the past tense of the verbs listed.

Presentation

1. Encourage students to do the exercise one sentence at a time so that they don't feel overwhelmed.

2. When students have finished, ask for volunteers to read sentences aloud. Set up a three-column chart on the board, with the headings *worked*, *decided*, and *learned*. As students read the sentences aloud, have a volunteer put the verb under the correct column according to the pronunciation.

Answers to Exercise 1

1. learned   2. moved   3. moved   4. played   5. moved   6. started

Person to Person

Preparation

1. Write the word *famous* on the board and display a newspaper or magazine picture of a famous person, the President of the United States, for example. Say that this person is *famous* and point to the word on the board. Ask students to define the word. Then ask them to give more examples.

2. If students are unfamiliar with the word, explain that *famous* means known about by many people.

Reading for Real

Preparation

1. Introduce the subject of the reading, Oprah Winfrey, by asking students what they already know about her. Write their responses on the board. If there are few or no responses, try these hints:

   - Have students look at Oprah's picture on page 41.
   - Draw the outline of a TV on the board. Pretend your pen is a microphone and go around asking questions to your "studio audience."

2. To introduce vocabulary, list these words on the board: *talk-show host, actress, TV news anchorperson, radio newscaster, producer, owner, studio,* and *radio station.* Give a definition and have students respond with the correct answer from the list.

   a. a person who gives the news on TV

   b. a person who gives the news on the radio

   c. a person who acts on TV or in the movies

   d. a person who owns something

   e. a person who makes TV shows and movies

   f. a person who interviews people

   g. a place where people on radio work

   h. a place where people on TV work

Presentation

Look at a United States map and point out these places where Oprah has worked: Nashville, Tennessee; Baltimore, Maryland; Chicago, Illinois.

Answers for Exercise 2

1. a. 1970   2. c. Tennessee, Maryland, and Illinois   3. b. Nashville

4. b. three years   5. a. starts with her present jobs

Answers to Talk About It

Oprah has three jobs now. She worked 15 years before she had her own show. Before Oprah was a talk-show host, she was a TV news anchorperson, TV reporter, TV news co-anchor, and radio newscaster.

In Your Experience

Preparation

1. Have students ask a student volunteer questions about his or her work history as you create her work history chart on the board.

2. Use this new chart to review the information students need in their own work histories. Leave it on the board as a model for students as they write their own histories.

Workbook

Workbook pages 19 and 20 can be assigned after students have completed Student Book page 39.

Page 42

Culture Corner

Preparation

1. Review the concept of working in groups or teams with designated roles by giving students an example of teamwork on the job: "In a fast-food restaurant, the cashier, the cooks, a manager, and others work at different jobs, but they work together. "Have students give you other workplace examples."

2. Ask students about teamwork at home or in their free time. For example, say, "In a family, the mother, father and children work together at home, but are their jobs at home all the same?" Then ask questions such as these:

   • What work do you do at home?

   • What does your husband or wife do?

   • What do your children do?

   • In your free time, if you play sports on a team, do all the teammates do the same job?

3. Write on the board the classroom-team roles given in Scene 1: *leader, secretary, time keeper* and *reporter.* Circle *leader.* Explain that the next activity in the book is about the leader's role on a team.

Presentation

1. Read through Culture Corner with the class. Work through the activities orally or have students individually write answers in their notebooks. Finish the entire page to check comprehension before assigning any group work.

2. Have students form groups. Write the classroom-team roles needed for the group activity on the board, such as *leader, secretary, time keeper,* and *reporter.* Give these instructions: "You have 20 minutes to work. You need to assign roles in your group and to write the roles on one piece of paper. Read page 42 again. Write the answers to all the exercises on the group paper. Report answers to me in 20 minutes. Begin."

3. Monitor and time groups.

4. Assess, with the class, the strengths and weaknesses of this group work activity after the 20 minutes elapse. Ask questions such as these:

   • Did your group finish?

   • Did everyone participate?

   • Did members work together?

5. Give your assessment. Tell students what you observed. Point out which groups were successful and why. Put special emphasis on any leadership skills that you observed. For example, point out those students who encouraged the group members to get started. Say, "I saw Juanita hold up a paper and ask her group for a volunteer secretary. She got the group started quickly."

Exercise 3

Preparation

To check comprehension of vocabulary, ask students to define and give examples of the words in the list, as well as *participating, share,* and *agree.*

Presentation

Remind students to get each group member's opinion on each sentence, not to do the exercise individually.

Answers to Exercise 3

1. ready   2. begin   3. understand   4. help   5. think   6. do

Activity Masters

Activity Master 4-1 can be assigned after students have completed Student Book page 42.

Preparation

1. Pre-teach new vocabulary from the reading: *civil war, fighting, died, calculator, homeless shelter, award, naturalized citizen.*

2. Make one copy of the handout for each student.

Presentation

1. Have students form into groups of four. (Smaller groups will have to take multiple group roles. Larger groups will have to share group roles or add additional roles, such as *dictionary checker,* for example.)

2. Give students instructions similar to those used for the small-group activity from Culture Corner, page 42. Give students a time limit of 30 or 40 minutes to assign roles and complete the activity. Additional instructions for the students are on Activity Master 4-1.

Page 43

Scene 2

Preparation

1. Write today's date on the board, but put the wrong day or year. Ask, "Is this correct?" When learners catch the mistake, respond by saying something like this:

   "Oops, I made a mistake. I didn't check my work. I need to correct my mistake."

   Write the words *mistake, check,* and *correct* on the board. Correct your mistake on the date. Use the vocabulary again as you change the date.

2. Tell students to check for a mistake in Scene 2.

Sound Bites

While You Listen

Presentation

1. Tell students that they will hear about one man, Bill Gates. Explain that you will play the tape three times and that they should try to listen for the specific information to answer the questions. Tell them that they do not have to write anything the first time they listen; they will write their answers when you play the tape the second time. When you play the tape the third time, they will check their answers.

2. Play the tape three times. When you play the tape the second time, students should mark their answers in their books. When you play the tape the third time, students should check their answers individually.

After You Listen

Presentation

After students have talked with a partner, discuss any problems with the class. You may wish to play the tape a fourth time to clarify the information for students.

Listening Script

1. Did Bill Gates grow up in Seattle, Washington?

   Yes, he did. He was born in Seattle, Washington, in 1955 and attended elementary and high school there.

2. Did Bill Gates attend college?

   Yes, he started to study in Harvard University in 1973, at the age of 18. He didn't finish college, though. He started his own company.

3. Did Gates develop computers?

   No, he developed software, the programs for computers. His company made software for IBM. This was quite an achievement.

Answers to Sound Bites

1. Bill Gates was born in Seattle, Washington.   2. He went to Harvard University.

3. He developed software for computers.

Activity Masters

Activity Master 4-2 can be assigned after students have completed Student Book page 43.

Preparation

Copy only one handout for each group. (Don't make copies for individual students.) Cut the sentences into strips ahead of time or have groups do so. Make sure each group also has a checklist from the bottom of the master.

Presentation

1. Tell learners that in this activity they will work in groups to correct mistakes in sentences.

2. Give directions and have one group model procedures before groups work independently.

3. Model taking turns. Have four students come to the front and sit in a circle. Have each take a sentence strip. Have one of the four students read aloud a sentence strip while the others listen. Explain to the class that each student's sentence will be the focus of the small group, one at a time.

4. Point out the checklist given to each group to help students locate the mistakes. Model using the checklist with a sentence containing mistakes on the board.

5. Explain that with 4 students in a group, each student can take two turns. If groups are larger or smaller, members can take turns until all sentences have been reviewed.

6. Read the directions on the group handout with the class and answer questions before groups work independently.

Page 44

Spotlight on Past Yes/No Questions and Negative Statements

Preparation

1. Ask several students what they did last week. Write their answers on the board. Here are some examples:

   - Nikolas visited the art museum last week.
   - Chi-Lin played baseball.
   - Talia painted her living room.

2. Model past-tense questions by asking another student about the examples on the board. Ask, "Did Nikolas visit the art museum?" When the student agrees, say, "Yes, he did." Write this response on the board next to the question. Continue with other students and other example sentences. Be sure to include questions that have negative responses.

Presentation

After students read the questions and answers in the Spotlight Box, ask additional questions that have negative responses, such as the following:

   - Did Bill Gates live in California?
   - Did he work for Apple Computers?
   - Did Sandra Cisneros work for a newspaper?

Exercise 4

Preparation

Have students read through the directions carefully to learn about Sandra Cisneros. You may wish to have one of her books on hand to show to the class.

Presentation

Before students begin, review the activity with the class to help students decide which blanks are for questions and which are for short answers.

Answers to Exercise 4

1. Did Cisneros come
2. didn't
3. Did she write
4. didn't
5. Did she stay
6. didn't

Workbook

Workbook page 21 can be assigned after students have completed Student Book page 44.

Page 45

Spotlight on Past Time Expressions

Preparation

1. Show a calendar to the class. Draw a calendar page of the current month on the board or project it on an overhead transparency.

2. Ask questions using the past time expressions presented in the Spotlight Box. Ask "What's today? What was yesterday? What was the day before yesterday?" etc. As students answer, write the expression on the appropriate date on the calendar.

3. Erase the expressions. Have volunteers point to the correct date as you call out an expression. Make the practice more competitive by dividing the class into teams to "race" to the board or to the overhead projector to point to the correct date.

Presentation

Introduce the expressions in the unit context by making a time line on the board similar to the one in the textbook, but label it with dates and events that are familiar to the students. Some events could be described as *started school*, or *finished vacation*, for example. Use the past time expressions to make sentences about past events and dates on the time line—for example, say, "We started school two months ago."

Exercise 5

Presentation

Go over the time line with the class. Be sure that students understand the concept of some events happening before others, but that every event happened in the past.

Exercise 6

Presentation

Have students read the first question. Ask someone to tell you what day it is. If he or she does not answer "October 30," explain that in the story Lisa is telling, it is October 30, so they should answer the questions as if it were that date today.

Answers to Exercise 6

1. last month   2. yesterday   3. three days ago   4. last week   5. two weeks ago

Workbook

Workbook page 22 can be assigned after students have completed Student Book page 45.

Get Graphic

Preparation

1. Have the class look again at the time line from the activity on the previous page. Ask students to explain what is different about the time line on page 46.

2. Review the meaning of *achievements*. Ask students if they can tell you about the achievements of these famous people just by looking at the pictures.

Presentation

Ask students to define and give examples of the following words: *illustrated time line, invented, Most Valuable Player, award, fiction, secretary of state*. Provide definitions for any words students do not understand.

Exercise 7

Preparation

If students do not already know what a medal is, explain the concept. Illustrate with available magazine photos of Olympic athletes.

Presentation

Point out that there is only one correct answer to each question.

Answers to Exercise 7

1. b.   2. c.   3. a.   4. c.

Exercise 8

Preparation

Elicit the definition of *quality* from the students. If no one can answer, say, "A quality is something that describes us as people. The word can also describe animals or things."

Page 48

Wrap-Up

Presentation

1. Display the illustrated time lines that the students made in the small-group activity on page 46 of Get Graphic. Review the parts to include when making an illustrated time line.

2. Give students a time limit of approximately 15 minutes to read and complete their time lines, and another 10 minutes to ask and answer questions with a partner.

Workbook

Workbook pages 23 and 24 can be assigned after students have completed Student Book page 48.

ANSWERS TO PROGRESS CHECKS

Progress Check A

Speak or Write

1. Oprah Winfrey and Bill Gates
2. Answers will vary. See Reading For Real, p. 41 and Wrap-Up, p. 48.
3. Answers will vary. See Sound Bites Scene 1 Script, p. 65.
4. Answers will vary. Here are some possible answers.
   I lived in Mexico for 18 years. I moved to the United States in 1996.

Listening Script

When Oprah was a young girl, she lived on her grandmother's farm. She played and worked on the farm. She didn't have many friends, so she talked to the animals! She liked to talk. At an early age, she wanted to speak in front of people. When she was only three years old, she practiced speaking at her church. People were surprised that Oprah was so good! At first, Oprah liked school, but when she moved from the farm to the big city, she changed. She didn't like to study. Oprah's father helped Oprah. Her father watched her do her homework. Now Oprah is a successful talk show host.

Listen

1. true   2. true   3. true   4. true   5. false   6. true

Progress Check B

Language Structures

Answers will vary. Here are some possible answers:

1. Bill Gates studied at Harvard University.
2. Gloria Estefan didn't live in China.
3. Roberto Clemente liked to help people.
4. Madeleine Albright didn't move to Czechoslovakia in 1997.
5. Martina Navratilova didn't practice to be a baseball player.

Questions

1a. Did Bill Gates study at Harvard University?
2b. Did Gloria Estefan live in China?
3c. Did Roberto Clemente like to help people?
4d. Did Madeleine Albright move to Czechoslovakia?
5e. Did Martina Navratilova practice to be a baseball player?

Content

1. d.   2. c.   3. a.   4. b.
5. false   6. true   7. false

ANSWERS TO ACTIVITY MASTERS

Activity Master 4-1

1. He was born in China in 1920.

2. His life was difficult. There were many problems in his country. His parents and sister died.

3. Answers will vary. Here are some possible answers:

   His problems made him stronger. He started Wang Laboratories and became a rich man. He helped people.

Activity Master 4-2

1. Gates, Washington
2. worked, Tennessee
3. baseball, helped
4. moved
5. invented, 1876
6. learned, Czechoslovakia
7. An Wang, started
8. worked

REPRODUCIBLE MASTER
UNIT 4

WORKBOOK ANSWERS

Practice 1

1. lived	5. liked	9. moved	13. talked
2. played	6. wanted	10. changed	14. tried
3. worked	7. practiced	11. helped	15. studied
4. talked	8. liked	12. watched	16. studied

Practice 2

1. started   2. lived   3. worked   4. lived   5. lived   6. changed   7. changed

Practice 3

1. Did Roberto Clemente play tennis?   2. No, he didn't.
3. Did An Wang start Microsoft?   4. No, he didn't.
5. Did Sandra Cisneros have her own TV show?   6. No, she didn't.

Practice 6

Time line

1954: Born in Chicago

1983: First book published

1991: Second book published

1992: Award for best fiction

Name _____ Date _____

PROGRESS CHECK A

SPEAK OR WRITE

Look at the pictures from Unit 4. Use the questions below to talk or write about each picture.

Questions

1. What successful people from Unit 4 do the pictures remind you of?

2. Tell about their achievements.

3. Name two other successful people from Unit 4, and tell about their past or their achievements.

4. Use these verbs to talk about your past: *live, move, start, work.*

LISTEN

While you listen, put a check under *True* or *False*.

	True	False
1. Oprah lived on a farm.	_____	_____
2. She talked to animals.	_____	_____
3. She started speaking at church.	_____	_____
4. She moved to the city.	_____	_____
5. Oprah's sister helped her to study.	_____	_____
6. Oprah is a successful talk-show host.	_____	_____

PROGRESS CHECK B

LANGUAGE STRUCTURES

Each sentence has a mistake. Cross out the mistake. Write the correct word or words above the sentence to make it true.

1. Bill Gates didn't study at Harvard University.

2. Gloria Estefan lived in China.

3. Roberto Clemente didn't like to help people.

4. Madeleine Albright moved to Czechoslovakia in 1997.

5. Martina Navratilova practiced to be a baseball player.

Now, make each sentence a question beginning with *did*.

1 a. _____? Yes, he did.

2 b. _____? No, she didn't.

3 c. _____? Yes, he did.

4 d. _____? No, she didn't.

5 e. _____? No, she didn't.

CONTENT

Match the leadership qualities with the correct meaning.

Leadership	Qualities	Meaning
1. _____	positive	a. works well with others
2. _____	hard-working	b. smart
3. _____	cooperative	c. not lazy
4. _____	intelligent	d. cheerful

True or False?

5. Teamwork skills are useful in schools and jobs, but not at home. _____

6. A work history gives information about job experience. _____

7. Only the teacher can correct mistakes. _____

ACTIVITY MASTER 4-1

Group Work: A Success Story and Questions

Take out one paper and write the name and role of each member of your group. Use these roles: leader, secretary, reporter, and time keeper. Read the story. Work as a team to write the answers to the questions on your group paper.

A Success Story: An Wang

An Wang was born in Shanghai, China, on February 7, 1920. His father was an English teacher. He started to teach his son English when An was only 4 years old. An was intelligent. He went to the university when he was 16 years old. He studied electrical engineering and English.

But An didn't have an easy life as a child. There were many problems in his country. China was having a civil war and also fighting with Japan. An Wang's parents died. His sister died too. But these problems made An a stronger person and helped him to succeed.

An Wang moved to the United States in 1945. He became a successful businessman. He started Wang Laboratories. The company made calculators and computer parts. An Wang became a rich man.

He liked to help people too. He gave money to schools and hospitals. He gave computers to a shelter for homeless people in New York City. He started a computer factory in Boston's Chinatown to make new jobs for people.

In 1986, An Wang received an award for being a outstanding naturalized citizen of the United States He died in 1990, but people will remember him as a very successful American.

Questions

Write answers on the group paper.

1. Where and when was An Wang born?

2. How was An Wang's life before he moved to the United States?

3. Give examples of An Wang's success.

REPRODUCIBLE MASTER
UNIT 4   ACTIVITY MASTER 4-2

Group Activity: Correct the Mistakes

There are two mistakes in every sentence. They may be mistakes in fact, spelling, grammar, capitalization, or punctuation. Each person in the group should take one sentence and correct it. Each student should then read the sentence to the group, explain the two mistakes and then review the corrections with the rest of the group. The group then agrees with the corrections or changes the corrections before moving on to the next sentence. (See the checklist to help you.)

✂ -

1. Bill gates was born in Ohio.

2. Oprah Winfrey works in Nashville, Maryland in 1983.

3. Roberto Clemente played basketball and helps many people before he died.

4. Gloria Estefan movied from Cuba to the United States in 1959?

5. Alexander Graham Bell inventid the telephone in 1976.

6. Martina Navratilova learns to play tennis in Cuba.

7. Bill Gates starting Wang Laboratories in 1951.

8. Madeliene Albright workt at the United Nations

✂ -

Checklist

Answer yes or no. Does the sentence have . . .

correct facts?

correct past tense?

correct spelling?

correct capitalization?

correct punctuation?

© NTC/Contemporary Publishing Group, Inc.

OVERVIEW

Objectives

Skills and Structures

Talk about people's problems

Listen to conversations

Understand a survey

Read a pie graph

Read about problems and solutions

Use a time line

Use direct object pronouns

Use count and noncount nouns

Use the future with *going to*

SCANS Competencies

Acquire and evaluate information: Student Book, Reading for Real, page 53

Make decisions: Workbook page 29; Activity Master 5-1.

Realia

A small jar filled with dried beans

A small jar filled with flour

ACTIVITY NOTES

Page 49

Scene 1

Preparation

Write the unit title on the board. Ask, "What do you think *shape up* means?" Have learners work in pairs or groups to prepare responses. Write their answers on the board or ask a learner to perform the task. If necessary, explain the topic.

Presentation

Ask questions about Scene 1.

- Who needs to exercise, Mark or Henri?

- What does Mark suggest? Does Henri agree?

- Why is Henri tired?

Sound Bites

While You Listen

Preparation

1. Ask students to define and give an example of *survey* and *habits*. If they are unable to do so, provide your own definitions and examples.

2. Have students review the Sound Bites chart. With the class, brainstorm examples of the types of information students will be asked to write in each column.

After You Listen

Preparation

Check students' understanding of *most* and *least* before placing them in small groups. Review if necessary.

Listening Script

Announcer:	We're doing a survey on exercise today. Callers, tell us your age, your form of exercise, and how often you exercise.
1. Female:	Hi, I'm 33 years old. I want to lose weight, so I exercise a lot. I ride my bicycle around the neighborhood. I ride it two times a week. There are a lot of hills, so it's hard work.
2. Male:	I'm 48. When I was younger, I played team sports—basketball and soccer. I don't play them much anymore. But now I go hiking in the mountains. I try to go every weekend.
3. Female:	Well, I'm 19 years old. I love rollerblading. I rollerblade in the park on Sunday. It's a great way to meet people, and it's good exercise too. I have my own roller blades. I bring them with me on vacation too.
4. Male:	Hello, I'm 25 years old. I take classes at a karate school four times a week. I like the self-discipline. I have my brown belt in karate now.
5. Female:	I'm 51, and I exercise almost every day. I take aerobics classes. I love it, and I feel great afterwards. The other days I jog. I feel bad if I don't exercise.

Answers to Sound Bites

Caller 1: riding bicycle, two times a week

Caller 2: hiking in mountains, every weekend

Caller 3: rollerblading, Sunday

Caller 4: karate, four times a week

Caller 5: aerobics classes almost every day, jogging the other days

Spotlight on Direct Object Pronouns

Preparation

1. Have one student stand in the front of the room across from you. Take an eraser from the board and toss it to them.

2. Ask the class, "Who threw the eraser? What did I throw? Who caught the eraser? What did he catch?" Explain that subjects do the action and direct objects receive the action. Write two sentences on the board about the demonstration. Say, for example, "I threw the eraser. [Name] caught the eraser." Ask volunteers to underline the subject and circle the direct object in each sentence. Have the class check the work for errors.

3. On the board in two vertical columns, write the subject and object pronouns as listed in the chart on page 51. Between the columns write the verb like or love.

4. Demonstrate the concept by writing sentences on the board. For example, write, "Maria loves her children" or "The students like their school."

5. Ask students to help you change the nouns to pronouns to make sentences such as "She loves them." or "They love it."

6. Erase *like* and *love* from the list on the board and write other verbs, such as *help, miss,* or *teach.* Have students work in pairs or groups to make more pairs of sentences, first using nouns, then changing the nouns to pronouns. Have several students write their sentences on the board for use in Exercise 1.

Presentation

Check comprehension of possible new words such as, *brown belt, get in shape,* and *conditioning machine* by asking questions such as the following:

- Is a brown belt for a beginner of karate or for an advanced student?
- Does *get in shape* mean "be healthy" or "make circles"?
- Is a conditioning machine for exercise or for working in the garden?

Answers to Exercise 1

Subjects	Direct Objects
Tina, she	aerobics, them
Mark, he	karate class, it
Victor, he	Marisa, her
Vera, she	Angelo, him
Our karate teacher, she	us, you, me

Exercise 2

Preparation

Have a volunteer read the first four sentences of Exercise 2. Ask the class to explain why it is the correct answer. Elicit from students that pronouns refer to nouns that have been mentioned in a previous sentence.

Answers to Exercise 2

1. it   2. him   3. him   4. them   5. it   6. it   7. us

Workbook

Workbook page 25 can be assigned after students have completed Student Book page 51.

Person to Person

Presentation

1. To check comprehension, ask questions, or have the students prepare and ask the class questions. Here are some examples:

   - What does Henri want to do?
   - What does Mark suggest to Henri?
   - What problem does Tina's father have?
   - Why doesn't Angelo exercise after work?
   - What does Victor tell Laura to do before she exercises?

2. Have students work in pairs to complete conversation 4. Ask pairs to present their conversations to the class.

Extension

Option 1: Students can perform the dialogues as written. You can assign pairs or let students choose their own partners.

Option 2: Students can make a simple substitution in some lines (by inserting different different health concerns and suggestions, for example).

Option 3: More advanced students can create additional conversations about health and exercise.

Reading for Real

Preparation

Remind students that they listened to other people take a survey in Sound Bites on page 50. Now they will be answering the questions for themselves.

Presentation

Emphasize that students should complete the survey with their own information.

Answers to Reading for Real

1. a   2. c   3. a   4. b   5. b

Talk About It

Extension

After students complete the Talk About It questions, have them write a paragraph describing their own health risks for heart disease.

Culture Corner

Presentation

1. Have students read the passage silently and circle words they don't understand.

2. Have students read alone, have them meet in groups to discuss words or phrases they don't understand.

3. After group discussion, have students ask you questions about any words or phrases they don't understand.

In Your Experience

Presentation

Ask learners to think of other questions they would like to ask in their groups. Invite volunteers to write a question on the board.

Extension

Have students write about what they learned in their group discussion. On the board write examples such as the following:

- There are four students in our group.

- Two of the students tried to lose weight before.

- The students in our group usually eat healthy food.

- In Liem's country some people go on diets when they have health problems. In his country, people do not usually go on diets to lose weight. They sometimes go on diets to gain weight.

Scene 2

Preparation

1. Have learners look at the pictures with a partner.

2. Help the pairs prepare questions to ask you about the pictures by writing sample questions such as these on the board.

- What does _____ mean?

- Would you explain _____ , please?

Presentation

Check comprehension by asking additional questions such as the following:

- What does *so sick* mean?

- What does *hurt all over* mean?

- What did Mark do when he *hung up?*

Extension

Option 1: Ask lower-level students to answer additional questions about Scene 2. Write one or more of the following questions on the board:

- What mistake did Mark make?
- What do you think the woman will do next?
- What can we learn from Scene 2?

Option 2: Students can create their own questions about the Scene, and have a partner answer them.

Option 3: More advanced students can write a story about Scene 2. Encourage them to use their answers to the questions as they write.

Sound Bites

Before You Listen

Preparation

Write the question "What reasons do people give for not coming to work?" on the board. Circle *reasons* and ask students to explain the meaning. (A reason explains *why*.)

Presentation

1. After students meet, have a reporter or secretary from each group report the group's answers by making a list on the board. Alternatively, a group secretary can write the list on a large paper during the discussion time. Another member can tape the paper on a classroom wall.

2. Discuss the lists. Have students identify which reasons are the same or almost the same and which ones are different. Ask them to identify which are good and bad reasons for not coming to work.

While You Listen

Preparation

1. Read the instructions for the exercise to the learners and check for comprehension. Ask questions such as the following:
   - Does *missing work* mean going to work or staying home?
   - Does *days off work* mean going to work or staying home?
   - What does *absent* mean?

2. Have small groups of students review the chart and brainstorm the types of information that they will be asked to write in each column.

After You Listen

Preparation

Review the correct answers with the class before having students compare them with the Before You Listen answers. You may wish to play the tape again to clarify anything students are having trouble with.

Listening Script

1. **George:**   This is Convex Hardware. George speaking.

   Henri: George, this is Henri Bouchart. I have a terrible cold, and I can't come in today.

   George: When are you going to come back?

   Henri: I'm going to return tomorrow. I just need a day to rest up.

2. **Secretary:**   Hathaway Elementary School.

   Vera: This is Vera Galvan, Ms. Delgado's instructional aide. Please tell Ms. Delgado I won't be in today.

   Secretary: What is the reason for the absence?

   Vera: My little girl has a sore throat. I'm going to take her to the doctor.

3. **Operator:**   Lind's Department Store. How may I direct your call?

   Victor: Furniture department, please.

   Salesman: Hello, furniture department. Ron speaking.

   Victor: Ron, this is Victor Ortiz. Please give a message to Mr. Rondel for me. My aunt died, and I'm going to Mexico for the funeral. I can't come to work this week, but I'm going to be back next Monday.

Answers to Sound Bites

Henri: cold, one day absent

Vera: sick daughter, one day absent

Victor: aunt died, one week

Page 56

Spotlight on Future with *Going to*

Preparation

1. Ask students questions such as the following:
   - What are you going to do after class today?
   - Are you going to exercise?
   - Who is going to cook something to eat?

2. On the board write sentences using the student information. Follow these examples:
   - José is going to read a book after class.
   - Lee and Martha are going to exercise.
   - Victor isn't going to exercise.
   - Muon and Mai aren't going to cook.

   Underline the verbs and *going to.*

3. On the board write, "I am going to exercise after class" along with the rest of the subject pronouns. Ask volunteers to write the rest of the conjugation on the board. Correct any errors with the class. Have students repeat the sentences after you.

4. Insert *not* in the first sentence and ask students to change the rest of the sentences again.

5. Repeat the exercise once more. This time have students replace the negative verbs with the appropriate contractions.

Exercise 3

Preparation

1. Have learners study the Exercise 3 directions and the sentences in the Spotlight Box. Ask pairs to make a list of words they don't understand.

2. Answer student questions about new words or direct the questions to the class for definitions or examples.

3. Check comprehension by asking these additional questions:
   - Is junk food good for your body?
   - Is an aerobics class an exercise class or a sport?
   - Are healthy actions things you think about or things you do?

Person to Person

Preparation

1. Read the first conversation to the class and explain the phrases *missing too much work* and *from now on*, if necessary.

2. Model the conversation again and have the learners repeat.

3. Have pairs of learners practice the conversation several times and then work together to practice and complete the second conversation.

4. Ask volunteers to present their new conversations to the class.

Workbook

Workbook pages 26 and 27 can be assigned after students have completed Student Book page 56.

Activity Masters

Activity Master 5-1 can be assigned after students have completed Student Book page 56.

Preparation

1. Explain that *take action* means to "do something." Then have students brainstorm actions they are going to take to improve their health.

2. On the board, write some examples of learner responses such as the following:
   - José is going exercise twice a week.
   - Maria is going to eat more fruits and vegetables.

Presentation

Have the learners practice the conversation at the top of Activity Master 5-1. Then model the activity by using a transparency of the activity or by writing a few sentences from the activity on the board.

Spotlight on Count and Noncount Nouns

Preparation

1. Introduce the concept of count and noncount nouns by playing a simple game. Fill a small jar with dry beans. Hold up the jar and ask, "How many beans do you think are in this jar?"

2. Invite students to write their names and guesses on small pieces of paper. Ask a student to collect all the papers.

3. Set up a committee to count the beans and announce the winner. (This can be done after class or at break time.) Announce the winner and perhaps offer a small prize.

4. Show students a small jar of flour. Ask, "How much flour is in this jar?" Choose volunteers to answer. If any of them answers correctly using measurement words, write that answer on the board.

5. Write the words *count* and *noncount* on the board. Write the word *beans* under *count*. Ask students to name other things we can count. Add them to the list.

6. Write the words *flour, time, water,* and *coffee* under *noncount*. Ask questions such as the following:

   • Do we count water or glasses of water?

   • Do we count coffee or cups of coffee?

   • How do we talk about time? Is our class for three time or three hours?

7. Ask students to name more noncount nouns and add them to the list.

Presentation

1. Read through the sentences in the Spotlight Box and the rules below them. Use a transparency and overhead projector, if available, to direct student attention.

2. On the board, write questions such as the following with the words from the *count* and *noncount* lists:

   • How much water do you drink every day?

   • How many glasses of water do you drink every day?

3. Ask students to come to the board to write the answers. Demonstrate correct answers such as the following:

   • I drink a little water every day.

   • I drink a lot of water every day.

   • I drink many glasses of water every day.

   • I drink a few glasses of water every day.

Exercise 4

Preparation

Have pairs of students classify the nouns in Exercise 4 as count or noncount before beginning the exercise.

Answers to Exercise 4

1. much   2. a little   3. many   4. a few   5. many   6. a few   7. a lot of   8. a little

Workbook

Workbook page 28 can be assigned after students have completed Student Book page 57.

Get Graphic

Preparation

Tell students to look at the graph. Elicit the reason it is called a pie graph, and the fact that in a pie graph all the percentages added together equal 100 percent.

Exercise 5

Preparation

Ask students to list the reasons for not coming to work and then to rank them in order from most common to least common.

Answers to Exercise 5

1. c   2. 82, 10, 6   3. a

Your Turn

Presentation

1. Have one group of students count the number of students currently in the class-room and report the number.

2. Have other groups of students prepare questions for the class. Appoint a secretary to write the questions on the board. Have students choose the questions they want to ask for the classroom survey. Here are some examples:

   • How many students were absent last month because of illness?

   • How many students were absent because of an illness in the family?

   • How many students were absent because of personal business?

   • How many students were absent because of a death in the family?

3. Appoint students to help conduct the classroom survey by doing the following: read the selected questions to the class, count hands as students respond to the questions, and record the numbers on the board as the counter reports. the sum of these numbers will represent the total number of students last month. Note that some students may have been absent more than one day, for several reasons. Other students may not have been absent at all last month. Therefore, the total number of reasons may be greater or fewer than the number of students in the class.

4. Have learners work in groups to determine, according to percentages of a whole, the reasons classmates were absent. Have each group make a pie graph following the example on page 58 in the Student Book, or on Activity Master 5-2.

5. Explain the math, if necessary. (Divide the number of students absent for each reason by the *total* number of reasons for absences. Example: Twelve students were absent due to personal business, so 12 divided by 48 *total* reasons for absences is .25 or 25%.
   Invite two group representatives to draw their group's pie graph on the board.

6. When all the graphs have been drawn on the board, have the class evaluate them for differences, similarities, and accuracy. Note: If figuring the math to make a pie graph is too difficult for your students, you may choose to have them do the exercise as a bar graph.

Activity Masters

Activity Master 5-2 can be assigned after students have completed Student Book page 58.

Presentation

1. To find the percentages of students who missed school for the reasons above, divide the number of students absent (105 due to illness) by the total number of students absent (150). The number 105 divided by 150 is .70, or 70%.

2. Write *illness* next to *70%* in the pie graph. Now find the percentage of students who were absent due to illness of a family member, personal business, and death in the family. Write the words in the correct places in the pie graph.

Page 59

Issues and Answers

Preparation

In small groups have students write a list of health questions they would like to ask a doctor. Tell groups to exchange lists with another group, and try to answer the other group's questions.

Presentation

1. Have students read the instructions, letters, and answers with a partner. Ask them to make a list of any words they don't understand.

2. Ask students to change partners and discuss the new words or phrases with the new partner. Then have them return to the first partner to share anything they have just learned.

3. Invite the class to ask you questions about any words that they still don't understand.

4. Check comprehension by asking questions or have students prepare questions to ask the class. Here are some possible questions:

   - What is Too Tired's problem?
   - Does Dr. Brownlee think naps will help Too Tired sleep better at night?
   - What is the problem for It Hurts?
   - What does the doctor think It Hurts should do about the headaches?

5. Have students share their ideas for Up in Smoke with other students. Invite a few volunteers to write their responses on the board. Ask questions like these about the writing to encourage student evaluation:

   - Do you like this idea?
   - Why do you think this is a good idea?
   - Is this a correct sentence?
   - Is the spelling correct?

Page 60

Wrap-Up

Preparation

1. Have students study the first paragraph and Mark's time line. Encourage them to ask about any words they don't understand.

2. Review Spotlight on the Future with *Going to*, if necessary.

Workbook

Workbook pages 29 and 30 can be assigned after students have completed Student Book page 60.

ANSWERS FOR PROGRESS CHECKS

Progress Check A

Speak or Write

Answers will vary. Here are some possible answers:

1. They are talking about exercise.

2. He is worried about his health.

3. No, he can't. He sold it.

4. No, he can't. He doesn't date her anymore.

5. I walk every day.

Listening Script

Answers are underlined.

Mark is (1) <u>worried</u> about his health. He (2) <u>misses</u> too much school because he is sick (3) <u>a lot</u>. He is going to (4) <u>take</u> action. He's (5) <u>going</u> to sleep more. He's also going to (6) <u>get</u> more exercise. He and his friend Vera (7) <u>are</u> going to go (8) <u>dancing</u> next Saturday. His doctor says he should stop eating (9) <u>junk</u> food. He's going to (10) <u>cook</u> healthy food tonight. He's going on a (11) <u>diet</u>, and he's going to (12) <u>try</u> to lose (13) <u>weight</u>.

Progress Check B

Language Structures

1. me	2. them	3. They	4. He
5. it	6. him	7. She	8. her

Content

1. F	2. T	3. T	4. F	5. T

ANSWERS FOR ACTIVITY MASTERS

Activity Master 5-1

Answers will vary. Students will fill in the blanks with classmates' names.

Activity Master 5-2

illness: 70%

illness of family member: 18%

personal business: 10 %

death in the family: 2%

WORKBOOK ANSWERS

Practice 1

1. it   2. her   3. you   4. us   5. it   6. them   7. me

Practice 2

1. He is going to use a sick day.

2. She is going to use a personal day.

3. They are going to use sick days.

4. She is going to use a personal day.

5. She is going to use a personal day.

6. They are going to use a vacation day.

Practice 3

1. I'm going to   2. I'm going to   3. I'm going to

4. is going to   5. She's going to   6. We're not going to

Practice 4

1. am going to visit   2. is going to take   3. are going to have   4. is going to visit   5. am going to cook   6. are going to come   7. are going to eat

Practice 5

1. many   2. a few   3. much   4. a little   5. a little (or a lot of)

6. many   7. a lot of

Practice 6

1. In week 1 Henri is going to sleep 7½ hours every night.

2. In week 2 Henri is not going to eat salty food or add salt to food.

3. In week 3 he is going to exercise. He's going to walk for 15 minutes two times a week.

4. In week 4 he isn't going to eat fried foods. He's only going to eat red meat twice a week.

REPRODUCIBLE MASTER
UNIT 5

PROGRESS CHECK A

SPEAK OR WRITE

Look at the pictures from Unit 5. Use the questions below to talk or write about each picture.

Questions

1. What are Henri and Mark talking about in these pictures?

2. What is Henri worried about?

3. Can Henri ride his bike? Why or why not?

4. Is Henri going to go dancing with Anne? Why or why not?

5. What kind of exercise do you do?

LISTEN

Listen and write the missing words.

Mark is (1) _____ about his health. He (2) _____ too

much school because he is sick (3) _____. He is going to

(4) _____ action. He's (5) _____ to sleep more. He's also

going to (6) _____ more exercise. He and his friend Vera

(7) _____ going to go (8) _____ next Saturday. His doctor

says he should stop eating (9) _____ food. He's going to

(10) _____ healthy food tonight. He's going on a (11) _____

and he's going to (12) _____ to lose (13) _____.

Name _____ Date _____

LANGUAGE STRUCTURES

Write the correct pronoun in the sentences. Use these words.

us   him   She   They   her   them   me   He

1. My diet helps _____ to lose weight

2. Mrs. Brown has 30 students. She helps _____ learn English.

3. Doctors know exercise is important. _____ tell us to exercise 20 minutes or more three times a week.

4. Mark plays soccer. _____ really likes it.

5. Tina takes aerobics classes. She takes _____ three times a week.

6. Martha cooks healthy food for her son. She doesn't give _____ junk food.

7. Mrs. Lopez is worried about her health. _____ has a history of heart disease.

8. Martin's daughter is six years old. He takes _____ to dance lessons.

CONTENT

Read the sentences. Put a check under *True* or *False*.

	True	False
1. Age is a risk factor you can control.	_____	_____
2. High levels of stress are a risk factor for heart disease.	_____	_____
3. Smoking is a risk factor you can control.	_____	_____
4. Cholesterol is good for your heart.	_____	_____
5. Men generally have heart disease at a younger age than women.	_____	_____

Name _____ Date _____

TAKE ACTION!

Read and practice this conversation with a partner.

Mark: I miss too much school because I get sick a lot.
      I'm going to do some things to have better health.

Vera: What are you going to do?

Mark: I'm going to sleep more every night.

Vera: That sounds like a good idea.

Walk around the room and ask other students questions.

What are you going to do to improve your health?

Are you going to _____?

Write the student's name next to the action he or she is going to take.

1. _____ is going to exercise more.

2. _____ is going to sleep more.

3. _____ is going to try to lose weight.

4. _____ is going to try to gain weight.

5. _____ is going to walk around the block every day.

6. _____ is going to stop eating junk food.

7. _____ is going to relax more.

8. _____ is going to ride a bike more often.

9. _____ is going to stop smoking.

10. _____ is going to _____.

11. _____ is going to _____.

MORE GRAPHIC SKILLS

There are 600 students at Midway Center Adult School. Last month 150 students missed one or more days of school. The students who were absent gave these reasons for missing school.

105 students were absent because of illness.

27 students missed school because of the illness of a family member.

15 students were absent because of personal business.

3 students were absent because of a death in the family.

Find the percentages. Write the reasons for absences in the correct places on the pie chart below.

Reasons for Absences at Midway Center Adult School

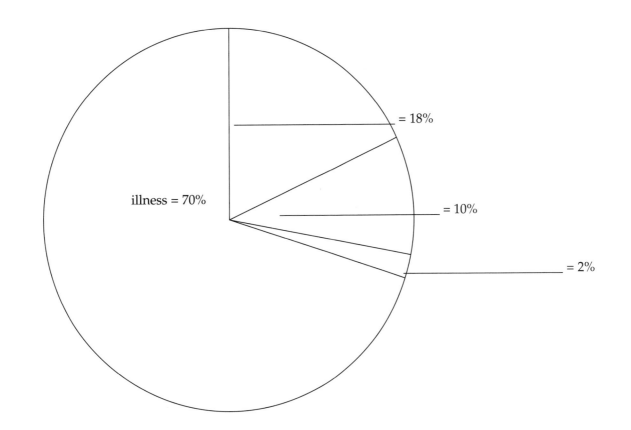

illness = 70%

= 18%

= 10%

= 2%

OVERVIEW

Objectives

Skills and Structures

Talk about people's problems

Understand housing ads

Read a chart

Read about reasons to rent or buy

Use an idea map

Use *how much/how many*

Use future with will

Use question words

SCANS Competencies

Serve clients or customers: Student Book, Culture Corner, page 66

Negotiate and arrive at decisions: Student Book, Scene 2, page 67

Evaluate information and make decisions: Activity Master 6-2

Realia

Rental ads from local newspaper

ACTIVITY NOTES

Page 61

Scene 1

Preparation

1. Write the title *Home, Sweet Home* on the board. Ask these questions about the title:

   - What do you think this unit is about?

   - Do you think the word "sweet" means nice or bad?

2. Have learners discuss the title in pairs or groups. Write discussion questions on the board or have students suggest questions. Here are some sample questions:

   - What makes your home a "sweet" or nice, place to live?

   - Do you live in an apartment or a house?

   - Did you live in an apartment or house in your country?

   - Is it easy or difficult to rent an apartment in this city?

   - Was it easy or difficult to rent an apartment in your country?

Presentation

Ask questions about Scene 1. Here are some examples:

   - In the first picture, what does Alex want to do?

   - In the second picture, why does the manager need to know if Alex has any pets?

   - Do you think Alex will get the apartment? Why or why not?

Extension

1. Have pairs create three additional questions about Scene 1.

2. Invite learners to write a few questions on the board. With the class check the questions for comprehension and accuracy. Have students evaluate the questions by asking the following questions:

   - Do you understand the question?
   - Is the spelling of the words correct?
   - Does every question have a question mark at the end and a capital letter at the beginning?
   - Is everything else correct?

3. Have learners work in pairs to answer the questions on the board. Invite volunteers to the board to write answers next to the questions. Again, check the students' work with the class by asking questions similar to those above.

4. Have students write a story about Scene 1.

Activity Masters

Activity Master 6-1 can be assigned now or anytime during the study of this unit.

Page 62

Sound Bites

While You Listen

Preparation

1. Write the words *Problem* and *Solution* next to each other on the board. Ask students for definitions or explain the words, if necessary.

2. Ask learners about a problem they might have with an apartment, or offer a problem of your own. Write a brief statement about it under *Problem.*

3. Ask learners for suggestions on how to fix the problem, and write a few of their answers under *Solution,* as shown here:

Problem	Solution
1. My rent is too expensive.	Get an extra part-time job.
	Move to a smaller apartment.
2. The neighbors are too noisy.	Call the manager.
	Talk to the neighbors.
	Call the police.

4. Ask learners for more examples of problems and solutions. Write them on the board or have a student perform the task for you.

After You Listen

Preparation

Review the correct answers with the class before placing students into groups.

Listening Script

Dan: What's the problem? You look depressed.

Alex: Oh, I'm just thinking about my apartment. It's so small. There's no room for me, my wife, my son, and all of our pets. Right now we have a one-bedroom apartment.

Dan: How many bedrooms do you need?

Alex: We need at least two.

Dan: Why don't you rent a bigger place?

Alex: We just don't have enough money.

Dan: How much more is the two-bedroom?

Alex: We need another $150 a month.

Dan: Well, what are you going to do?

Alex: I'm thinking about getting another job on the weekends. Then we'd have extra money for rent.

Answers to Sound Bites

1. It's too small.
2. He wants two bedrooms.
3. He doesn't have enough money.
4. He is going to get a part-time job.

Page 63

Spotlight on *How Much* and *How Many*

Preparation

1. Review count and noncount nouns. Write the words *count* and *noncount* next to each other on the board. Ask students to give examples. Have a student volunteer write the words on the board in the appropriate lists.

2. If necessary, review the concept that *money* is a *noncount* word. We count *dollars* and *cents* when we talk about money.

Exercise 1

Preparation

Ask students to define *current* and *previous*. If they are unable to do so, provide a definition.

Exercise 2

Preparation

After students have read the application, clarify any words they do not understand.

Presentation

Remind students that this exercise has two parts. They also need to use the application to answer the questions in their notebooks.

Answers to Exercise 2

1. many / She was at her address for one year.

2. much / She has $980 dollars in the bank.

3. many / She was at her job for five months.

4. many / She has two children.

5. many / She has one job.

Workbook

Workbook page 31 can be assigned after students have completed Student Book page 63.

Page 64

Person to Person

Preparation

1. Review the term *security deposit* if necessary.

2. Read the first paragraph of Person to Person to the learners.

3. To encourage them to ask questions about new or difficult words, write a sample question like, "What does _____ mean?" on the board.

4. Have other learners volunteer definitions in response to the questions, or offer your own.

5. Check comprehension of the initial paragraph by asking questions.

Extension

Option 1: Lower-level learners can answer the following questions about the dialogues with a partner:

- How much is the security deposit for Lisa's apartment?

- How does Lisa feel about the security deposit?

- How many pets does Alex have?

Option 2: Have pairs of learners work together to write questions about the conversations. Circulate and check questions. If some students have difficulty writing questions, look for some good student models and ask writers to present their questions to the class, or write them on the board. Have students find new partners and practice the questions and answers with different learners.

Option 3: More advanced learners can create additional dialogues about renting an apartment in pairs and present them to the class.

Page 65

Reading for Real

Preparation

Hold up a page of housing ads from your local paper. Ask questions like these to stimulate interest and introduce vocabulary.

- What's this?
- Do you ever read ads to learn about apartments for rent?
- Did you find your apartment or house in the newspaper?
- How did you find your apartment?

Extension

1. For additional conversation practice have learners work in groups to discuss and evaluate the ads on this page as possible new homes for Alex. Ask them to discuss what's good and what's bad about each place.

2. Have groups prepare questions that Alex needs to ask about each ad. Here are some examples:

- Are pets OK?
- Is there a deposit?
- How much is it?

3. Have groups decide if one of these places might be good for Alex, or if he needs to look some more.

4. Have volunteers from each group report the group's decisions and questions for Alex.

Exercise 3

Preparation

Ask students to give examples of *most expensive, least expensive. location,* and *local.* Define and give examples of any words they don't understand from the ads

Answers to Exercise 3

1. c	2. a	3. c	4. a	5. c

Activity Masters

Activity Master 6-2 can be assigned after students have completed page 65.

Page 66

Culture Corner

Preparation

1. Introduce the concept of performing a task by writing the following chart heading on the board: *Steps to Follow to Rent an Apartment.*

2. Explain that steps to follow are things you need to do to complete a task, in the order you need to do them. Then ask students to give you ideas about things you need to do to rent an apartment. Write a list on the board or ask a student to do it for you. Have students copy the list.

3. Have learners work in pairs or groups to number the list in the order that the things need to be done. Prepare students for activity by asking them to think about questions such as

- What do you need to do first?
- What do you need to do second?
- What do you need to do next?

4. Have a volunteer rewrite the list as the class gives information about the order. A final list might look like the following:

   1. Read ads.
   2. Call the telephone numbers in the ads and ask questions.
   3. Go to see some apartments.
   4. Read and sign papers.
   5. Pay rent and security deposit.

5. Tell students that they will be reading the steps involved in starting a home day-care business.

Extension

In pairs, have students compare the steps in the Preparation activity with the steps in starting a daycare. Which task do they think is more difficult? Why?

Page 67

Scene 2

Presentation

1. Have students make guesses about the content and vocabulary in Scene 2 by asking questions such as the following:

   - What are these people talking about?
   - Why do you think Linda is going to call the real estate agent?
   - What do you think *make an offer* means?
   - What do you think *sold* means?
   - Do you think Linda and her husband are going to buy this house?

2. Give learners time to study Scene 2 and the questions that follow in pairs or groups.

3. Check comprehension by giving definitions or examples of key vocabulary and asking students to identify words from Scene 2. Here are some examples:

   - A person who helps people buy and sell houses is a _____ _____ _____. (real estate agent)
   - When a person buys a house, we say the house is _____. (sold)
   - When a person says, "I want to buy the house and I will pay $100,000 for it," he or she _____ _____ _____. (makes an offer)

Extension

Have pairs of students role-play the Scene in one of several ways. Bring in props or costumes to make the activity more interesting.

 Option 1: Students can perform the lines as written. You can assign pairs or let students choose their own partners.

Option 2: Students can make a simple substitution in some lines (by inserting a different address or area for example).

Option 3: More advanced students can ad-lib a conversation on the topic treated in the Scene or imagine they are in the conversation.

Sound Bites

Before You Listen

Presentation

1. To help learners focus on content, not grammar, have them discuss the pre-listening questions *without* writing answers. You can give these directions: Put your pencils on the table. Now meet with your partner (or group) and talk about the questions.
2. Have students report answers to the pre-listening questions.

While You Listen

Preparation

1. Have students copy the questions in their notebooks.
2. Remind students that long answers are not necessary for listening exercises. They should listen for names, times, and locations, and then write them quickly.

After You Listen

Preparation

Have students report answers to the class. With the class discuss what real estate agents do on a daily basis. List the activities on the board for students to refer to during group discussion.

Extension

 Option 1: Lower-level students can dictate a story about what happens to Linda and her real estate agent when they go to look at houses. Tell them to use Scene 2 and their listening notes as a guide. Write their ideas on the board.

Option 2: Have students write a continuation of the dialogue between Linda and her real estate agent from the Sound Bites. They can practice their dialogue and perform it in front of the class.

Option 3: More advanced students can pretend they are Linda, and write a description of her perfect home.

Listening Script

Narrator:	The real estate agent is going to help the Browns look for another house.
Linda:	I'm so upset about the house on Orange Avenue. We really liked that house.
Patty:	There are more houses. Maybe you'll find one you like more.
Linda:	Maybe.
Patty:	We'll look at more houses soon. Do you want to make an appointment?

Linda:	Let me think. We'll be away on Sunday. How about Saturday in the afternoon?
Patty:	Fine. Is 2:00 a good time for you?
Linda:	That'll be fine.
Patty:	Meet me at the real estate office. We'll use my car.

Answers to Sound Bites

Answers will vary. Here are some possible answers.

1. Linda wants to make an appointment.

2. She wants to look at houses.

3. They are going to meet at Patty's real estate office on Saturday afternoon at 2:00.

Page 68

Spotlight on Future with *Will*

Preparation

1. Introduce this grammar point by asking questions about what the learners *will* do after class and by writing short response sentences such as the following on the board:

   - José will go to work after class.
   - Maria and Mai will cook dinner tonight.

2. Demonstrate the negative form of the verb by asking more questions like the ones below until you get a negative response.

   - Samir, will you go to work after class?
   - How about you, Victor? Will you go to work after class?

3. As negative responses are given, write appropriate short sentences on the board. Here are some examples:

   - Samir and Victor will not go to work after class.
   - Veronica will not cook dinner tonight.

4. Underline *will* and the verb in each sentence to demonstrate how the future is formed.

5. Erase the names from each sentence. Have learners suggest appropriate pronouns to replace names.

6. Erase *will* and *will not* from each sentence and replace them with the appropriate contractions. Some final sentences on the board might be the following:

   - He'll go to work after class.
   - They'll cook dinner tonight.
   - They won't go to work after class.
   - She won't cook dinner tonight.

Exercise 3

Presentation

When students have completed the exercise, have them orally compare answers with a partner. Circulate to listen for pronunciation difficulties.

Answers to Exercise 3

Answers will vary. Here are some possible answers.

1. will look at	2. will go	3. will meet	4.will be
5. will go	6. won't drive	7. will see	8. won't look at

Person to Person

Presentation

Check comprehension by asking questions such as the following:

- Does the owner already have the house or does he want to buy it?
- Does "offer $98,000" mean you buy the house for $98,000, or that you want to buy the house for $98,000?

Workbook

Workbook page 32 can be assigned after students have completed Student Book page 68.

Page 69

Spotlight on Wh- Question Words

Preparation

1. Introduce this lesson by asking questions using Wh- question words. Here are some examples:

   - Where are you from?
   - When does class begin?
   - Why do you come to class?
   - What's your telephone number?
   - Who is your teacher?
   - How do you come to school?

2. As you ask each question, write only the question word on the board.

Presentation

1. Read the examples on page 69 in the Student Book and have students repeat them after you.

2. Check comprehension by presenting examples or have learners create the questions. Here are some examples:

   - When we want information about a person or people, we use the question word _____. (who)
   - When we want information about things such as a telephone number or address, we use the question word _____. (what)
   - When we want to know about the reason a person does something, we use the question word _____. (why)
   - When we want information about the way a person does something, for example, the way he goes to work, we use the question word _____. (how)

Answers to Exercise 4

North Park House

1. Sunday 1:00–5:00
2. North Park
3. Ofelia Gomez
4. It has a fireplace and a patio.
5. Call Ofelia Gomez at Arrow Realty

Blue Lake Townhouse

1. Sunday 1:00–4:00
2. Near Blue Lake
3. Dora
4. It's quiet, and it has a view, and a garage.
5. Call Dora at Arrow Realty

Your Turn

Presentation

Remind students to answer questions based on the new ads their partner has given them, not the ads in Exercise 4.

Workbook

Workbook pages 33 and 34 can be assigned after students have completed Student Book page 69.

Page 70

Get Graphic

Preparation

1. Ask these questions:
   - Do you own your home, or do you rent?
   - Do you want to buy a home some day?
   - Is it easier to buy a home in the United States or in your native country?
   - Do you think it's more expensive to buy a home or to rent? Why?

2. If necessary, present a short explanation of *higher, the highest, lower* and *the lowest*. You can do this by drawing two houses on the board. Identify them as *House A* and *House B*. Write *$85,000* under House A and *$95,000* under House B. You can then write *lower cost* and *higher cost* next to the appropriate prices, or have a student write for you.

3. To demonstrate the meaning of *the lowest* and *the highest*, draw one more house on the board, label it *House C*, and write *$105,000* under it. Under house C you can now write *the highest cost*, and under House A you can add *the lowest cost*. Or you could ask a learner to perform this task for you.

Presentation

Ask students to read the headings on the chart. Check comprehension by asking questions or having learners fill in statements about the houses. For example,

- The price of a home in the middle between the highest and lowest costs is the _____ _____ _____ _____ _____ (average cost of a home)
- The percent of money I pay to the bank when I borrow to buy a house is the _____ _____ _____ (home loan rate)
- The money I pay to the bank every month when I buy a house is the _____ _____ _____ (monthly mortgage payment)

Answers to Exercise 5

1. c   2. c   3. a   4. b   5. c

Issues and Answers

Preparation

Find out how many students rent an apartment and how many own a home. Divide the class in half according to students' situations and have them discuss the thing they like most and the thing they like least about owning or renting.

Presentation

Have students write the two additional entries for each list individually. Encourage students to be creative.

Extension

For additional writing practice have learners write one paragraph about reasons to buy a house and another about reasons to rent an apartment.

Wrap-Up

Presentation

Encourage learners to inquire about any of unit components that may be unclear to them by writing examples of questions on the board such as the following:

- Will you explain _____ again, please?
- Where can I review the lesson about _____?

Workbook

Workbook pages 35 and 36 can be assigned after students have completed Student Book page 72.

ANSWERS TO PROGRESS CHECKS

Progress Check A

Speak or Write

Answers will vary. Here are some possible answers.

1. They are talking about buying a house.
2. Patty is a real estate agent.
3. The house is already sold.
4. She is upset.

Listening Script

Manager:	Northside Apartments
Alex:	This is Alex Costa. I'm calling about your ad in the paper.
Manager:	How can I help you?
Alex:	How much is the two-bedroom apartment?

Manager:	It's $750 a month.	
Alex:	And what about the security deposit?	
Manager:	That's $500.	
Alex:	OK. And what about the electricity? Do I pay extra for that?	
Manager:	No, you don't. The electricity is included.	
Alex:	Sounds good. When can I see it?	
Manager:	I'll be here after 5:00 tomorrow evening.	
Alex:	Tomorrow is Saturday. I can come around 6:00.	
Manager:	Fine. I'll see you Saturday at 6:00.	
Manager:	Good afternoon. Orange Glen. How can I help you?	
Alex:	This is Alex Costa. I'm calling about the two-bedroom apartment. Can you tell me how much the rent is?	
Manager:	Sure. It's $825 a month.	
Alex:	And the security deposit?	
Manager:	$575. You also have to pay for the electricity every month. It's not included.	
Alex:	That's a lot of money, but I'd like to see the apartment. Can I make an appointment for Tuesday? It's my day off.	
Manager:	No problem. Is 10:00 good for you?	
Alex:	Yes, 10:00 is good. See you Tuesday.	

Listen

Information	Northside Apts	Orange Glen
Rent	$750	$825
Security Deposit	$500	$575
Electricity included?	yes	no
Appointment day and time	Sat. / 6:00	Tues. / 10:00

Progress Check B

Language Structures

1. What   2. Who   3. Where   4. When   5. How

Content

1. c   2. e   3. b   4. g   5. d

6. f   7. a

ANSWERS TO ACTIVITY MASTERS

Activity Master 6-1

Answers will vary.

Activity Master 6-2

1. The rent is $700 a month.

2. The rent is $775 a month.

3. He will need to pay $1,250 before he moves in: $450 for the security deposit, $700 for the first month's rent, plus $100 for his two dogs.

4. He will need to pay $1,275.

5. The apartment at Orange Glen will be more expensive.

6. The Paradise Garden apartment is near a bus or train stop.

7. The Orange Glen apartment has a swimming pool. It is near a school and a park.

8. Answer will vary. Here is a possible answer:

   I think Alex should rent the Paradise Garden apartment because it is cheaper and it is near transportation.

REPRODUCIBLE MASTER
Unit 6

WORKBOOK ANSWERS

Practice 1

1. How much   2. How much   3. How many

4. How many   5. How much   6. How much

Practice 3

1. Habitat for Humanity

2. Orange County, California

3. The old house was too small.

4. The Martinez family and volunteers.

5. People who work without pay.

Practice 4

1. Where's   2. Who's   3. When's   4. What's

Practice 5

1. The townhouse is near downtown.

2. The open house is Sunday from 12:00–4:00.

3. Call Ofelia Gomez.

4. The townhouse is $185,000.

Name _____ Date _____

SPEAK OR WRITE

Look at the pictures from Unit 6. Use the questions below to talk or write about each picture.

Questions

1. What are the Browns talking about in the first picture.

2. What's the problem in the second picture?

3. What do you think Patty's job is?

4. How do you think Linda Brown feels in the second picture?

LISTEN

Alex is looking for a new apartment. He reads the ads in the newspaper and calls about two of them. He talks to the manager at *Northside Apartments* and also to the manager of the apartments at *Orange Glen*. Listen to the conversations. Write the information in the chart.

Information	Northside Apts.	Orange Glen
Rent		
Security Deposit		
Electricity Included?		
Appointment Day and Time		

PROGRESS CHECK B

LANGUAGE STRUCTURES

Write the correct word in the questions below. Use the words below.

How   What   Who   When   Where

1._____ do the Browns want to buy?   A house.

2._____ is the real estate agent?   Patty is.

3._____ will Linda look at houses?   In the North part of town.

4._____ is her appointment?   At 2:00 on Saturday.

5._____ will Linda get to Patty's office?   She'll drive.

CONTENT

Match the words with the meanings. Write the correct letter next to the number.

_____ 1. real estate agent

_____ 2. BA

_____ 3. BR

_____ 4. unfurn.

_____ 5. incl.

_____ 6. mortgage payment

_____ 7. make an offer

a. say how much you'll pay for a house.

b. bedroom

c. person who helps people buy and sell homes.

d. You don't pay extra money.

e. bathroom

f. money paid every month to the bank for the loan on your house

g. no furniture

Name _____   Date _____

LET'S TALK ABOUT HOMES

Talk to two other students about their houses or apartments. Fill in the chart below with information about your partner's home and about your home.

Questions	Partner #1	Partner #2	You
Do you live in an apartment or house?			
How many bedrooms does it have?			
Is it big enough for you?			
Do you have a garage or a reserved parking space?			
What do you like about your home?			
Is there something you want to change or fix in your apartment or house?			
What is it?			

Now write about you. In your notebook, write a paragraph about your apartment or house. Use the information above.

MORE READING FOR REAL

Alex needs a new apartment because the apartment he has now is too small for his wife, his son and all of his pets. His family has eight pets! They have two dogs, three fish, a bird and two pet mice. They have a one-bedroom apartment, but they need at least a two-bedroom apartment. The location is important because the family doesn't have a car. Yesterday Alex cut these two ads from the newspaper.

Paradise Garden Apartments	Orange Glen
2 BR 2BA Unfurn a/c	2BR 1BA Unfurn
$700 mo $450 sec dep	Nr schools & park
elec and water incl	$775 mo sec dep $500
add'l $50 for ea dog/cat	water incl/elec not incl
Nr shopping and trans	pets OK Pool
221-456-8765	221-435-9887

Work together in a group. Read the ads and answer the questions. Then talk about the ads. Which apartment do you think Alex should rent?

1. How much is the rent for the Paradise Garden Apartment?

2. How much is the rent for the apartment at Orange Glen?

3. How much money will Alex need to pay before his family moves into the Paradise Garden apartment?

4. How much money will he need to pay to move into the apartment at Orange Glen?

5. Which apartment will be more expensive every month?

6. Which apartment is near transportation?

7. Which apartment has good things for Alex's son?

8. Which apartment do you think Alex should rent? Why?

OVERVIEW

Objectives

Skills and Structures

Talk about getting around

Read about a bus driver's job

Report an accident

Learn about rules for cars

Read a train schedule

Complete a T-chart

Use *have to* and *need to*

Use present continuous

Use *could* and *would* for requests

SCANS Competencies

Allocate money: Student Book, Get Graphic, page 82

Demonstrate responsibilities: Student Book, Spotlight on *Need to* and *Have to,* page 75

Realia

Several copies of the driver's test information booklet for your state

ACTIVITY NOTES

Page 73

Scene 1

Preparation

1. Introduce the topic of this unit by asking questions such as the following about learners' previous experiences:

   - How do you come to school?

   - How long does it take you to come to school?

2. If necessary, explain that the idiom *it takes 20 minutes* means "I/You need 20 minutes."

   - Do you spend more time getting around in this city, or did you spend more time getting around in your native country? (This is a good time to write the unit title, *Getting Around* on the board.)

   - What does *getting around* mean?

   - Is transportation in the United States more expensive or less expensive for you than in your country?

   - Is it easy or difficult for you to get around in this city?

   - What problems do you have getting around in this city?

Presentation

Check comprehension by giving definitions or examples and asking students to identify the words. Here are some examples:

- The money we pay to ride a bus is a _____. (fare)
- The money a cashier returns to us when we pay too much is _____. (change)
- When the bus driver cannot give us money back, he says we need to have _____ _____. (exact change)
- When we have a lot of problems doing something, we say it's a _____. (hassle)

Extension

Have pairs of students role-play the Scene for the class in one of several ways. Bring in props or costumes to make the activity more interesting.

Option 1: Students can perform the lines as written. You can assign pairs or let students choose their own partners.

Option 2: Students can make a simple substitution in some lines (by changing the fare or inserting the name of a local store, for example).

Option 3: More advanced students can ad-lib a conversation on the topic treated in the Scene, or imagine they are in conversation with the characters in the Scene.

Activity Masters

For further conversation about the learners' experiences with transportation, Activity Master 7-1 can be assigned now, or at anytime during the study of this unit.

Page 74

Sound Bites

While You Listen

Preparation

Before playing the tape, have students read the questions and answer any questions they have.

Presentation

1. Tell students that they will hear three conversations. Explain that you will play the tape three times and that they should try to listen for the specific information to answer the questions. Tell them that they do not have to write anything the first time they listen; they will circle their answers when you play the tape the second time. When you play the tape the third time, they will check their answers.

2. Play the tape three times. When you play the tape the second time, students should mark their answers in their books. When you play the tape the third time, students should check their answers individually.

After You Listen

Presentation

1. Have students work in pairs to compare their answers. Circulate among the students and answer any questions they may have.

2. Go over the correct answers with the class.

3. If necessary, play the tape a fourth time to clarify any parts that students may have found difficult.

Listening Script

1. Operator: Hello. Regional Transit Center.

   Ivan: Yes. I need to go downtown.

   Operator: Where are you going?

   Ivan: I'm going to 4515 Market Street.

   Operator: Where are you now?

   Ivan: I'm on Vermont Street.

   Operator: What's the cross street?

   Ivan: Excuse me?

   Operator: What street crosses Vermont Street at the corner?

   Ivan: Oh, I don't know, but the address is 615 Vermont.

   Operator: Let's see. You need to take bus 24.

   Ivan: Bus 24? Thank you.

2. Bart: Hanna, how much is the bus?

   Hanna: You have to have a dollar and 75 cents.

   Bart: I have two dollars.

   Hanna: You have to get exact change.

   Bart: Does the bus driver give change?

   Hanna: No way!

3. Marta: Here's my money, $1.75. And I need a transfer to bus 10 at Imperial Avenue.

   Driver: Then you have to pay another 35 cents.

   Marta: Here you go. Do I have to pay again on bus 10?

   Driver: No, give the transfer to the driver.

   Marta: I got it. Thanks.

Answers to Sound Bites

Conversation 1:	1. no	2. yes	3. no
Conversation 2:	4. no	5. no	
Conversation 3:	6. yes	7. yes	

Spotlight on *Need to* and *Have to*

Preparation

1. Introduce this grammar point by making a statement about yourself with *need to,* and then writing it on the board. Some possible introductory statements might be the following:
   - I need to buy gas for my car after school today.
   - I need to buy some food before dinner tonight.

2. Demonstrate that *need to* and *have to* are similar in meaning by erasing *need to* in each sentence and replacing it with *have to.* Apply the concept to the lives of the learners by asking questions about need, such as the following:
   - What do you need to do after class today?
   - What do you have to do before dinner tonight?

3. Write statements about the learners on the board or ask students to do it for you.

4. Have the students read the statements after you. Underline *need to* or *have to* in each sentence. Make sure some sentences have singular nouns and others have plural nouns. Here are some examples:
   - Muon needs to take his wife to the doctor.
   - Mohammed has to fix his car.
   - Maria and Sophia have to go shopping for food.

5. Elicit negative responses by asking specific questions such as the following:
   - José, do you have to buy gas for your car after school today?
   - Martin and Luisa, do you need to buy food before dinner tonight?

6. Write the negative sentences on the board.

7. Again, have learners repeat the sentences after you. Underline *doesn't* or *don't* and *need to* or *have to* in each sentence.

Presentation

1. Read the words in the Spotlight Box. Have the learners repeat them.

2. Check comprehension by erasing the verbs in the sentences you wrote on the board in the Preparation section. Then have learners volunteer to fill in the missing words. For example, the sentences above now would appear as shown here:
   - Muon _____ _____ take his wife to the doctor.
   - Mohammed _____ _____ fix his car.
   - Maria and Sophia _____ _____ buy food.
   - José _____ _____ _____ buy gas. (negative)
   - Martin and Luisa _____ _____ _____ buy food. (negative)

3. Provide additional practice by having volunteers change *need/needs to* to *have/has to* in each sentence on the board.

4. You can also ask learners to go to the board and change the positive sentences to negative and vice versa.

Extension

1. For additional conversation practice have partners discuss what they need to do after school. Write one or two questions on the board or ask a learner to perform the task for you. Here are some examples:
   - What do you need to do after class today?
   - What do you have to do before dinner tonight?
2. Have students report their partners' answers to the class.
3. For additional writing practice have students write three sentences about themselves and three sentences about their partners with *need to* and *have to*.

Exercise 1

Preparation

1. Have students look at the illustration and guess what the story will be about before they read it.
2. Tell students to define and give examples of the following vocabulary: *traffic, transfer, passengers,* and *responsible*. If students are unable to define these words, provide definitions.

Workbook

Workbook pages 37 and 38 can be assigned after students have completed Student Book page 75.

Page 76

Person to Person

Presentation

1. Read or play the first conversation while the students listen. Then read it again and have them repeat after you. Check comprehension by asking questions such as the following:
   - Are there any words you don't understand?
   - What is Pablo's problem?
   - What does he need to do?
   - Who do you think Mr. Smith is?
2. Follow the steps above for conversations 2 and 3. Here are some possible questions to ask to check comprehension:

   Conversation 2
   - Do you think Martin and Pablo are friends?
   - Where did Pablo need to go? Why?
   - Where's the pharmacy?

   Conversation 3
   - What did Pamela ask Mark?
   - What did Mark say to Pamela?
   - What did Pamela need to do before she can give Mark five dollars for gas?
3. Have partners study conversation 4 and create an ending for it. Then have learners present their conversations to the class.

Reading for Real

Preparation

1. Ask students to brainstorm a list of information that they might be asked to give on a car accident report. Write their ideas on the board for students to refer to while they are reading.

2. Ask students if they know what an insurance card is and why they should carry one. Explain the rules in your state about car insurance coverage.

Exercise 2

Presentation

After learners write the answers, have them close their notebooks and practice the conversation. Only the student playing the role of the police officer should refer to the Student Book in order to ask the questions. Have pairs present their conversations to the class.

Extension

Ask a learner who has had an accident to volunteer to discuss it with the class. Have the class ask questions about the accident. They can refer to the list of ideas on the board for what kinds of questions they need to ask.

Answers to Exercise 2

Answers will vary. Possible answers include:

1. Yes, officer, here it is.

2. No, no one was hurt.

3. I hit the rear end of his car.

4. It happened at 1:30 A.M.

5. The accident was on Lemon Street in Dallas, Texas.

Culture Corner

Presentation

1. For ESL classes in a state other than California, ask students to compare your state's driving rules with those of California. Are they the same or different?

2. For ESL classes in California, ask students to work in pairs to prepare questions about the reading. Here are some possible questions:

   • Do three-year-old children need to sit in a child safety seat?

   • What does the breath test check for?

Scene 2

Preparation

Discuss any unfamiliar terms in Scene 2, such as *on the hour* or *hate*. Check comprehension by asking questions such as the following:

- The bus comes at 1:15.
- Is that "on the hour"?
- Does *hate* mean "like very much" or "not like at all"?

Sound Bites

Before You Listen

Presentation

1. Give pairs a five-minute time limit to make this list.
2. Ask students to define and give examples of sentences with the following words: *convenient, costs less,* and *repairs*. Provide definitions for any of these words that students do not know.

While You Listen

Presentation

1. Tell students that they will hear one conversation. Explain that you will play the tape three times and that they should try to listen for the specific information in their lists. Tell them that they do not have to write anything the first time they listen; they will write their answers when you play the tape the second time. When you play the tape the third time, they will check their answers.
2. Check comprehension by asking questions such as the following:
   - What kind of transportation does Bassam think costs less?
   - What kind of transportation has expensive repairs?
   - What kind of transportation does Bassam's friend think is convenient?

Extension

Have learners work in groups to think of additional pros and cons about different kinds of transportation. Have groups report their ideas to the class. For additional writing practice, have students write their ideas about the different kinds of transportation in paragraph form.

After You Listen

Presentation

You may want to organize a small debate about whether or not your city has enough public transportation, and which kind of public transportation is best.

Listening Script

1. **Bassam:**   Jamal, are you driving to work today?

   Jamal: Yes, and I have to leave in two minutes.

   Bassam: Are you going past the post office?

   Jamal: Yes, that's my usual route. Why?

   Bassam: Well, could you give me a ride? My car's in the shop. I took the bus yesterday, but I got to work late.

   Jamal: Sure, no problem. So what happened to your car?

   Bassam: It just needs some repairs. But it's going to cost $250.00.

   Jamal: That's expensive!

   Bassam: Yes, cars are expensive to repair. Public transportation costs so much less.

   Jamal: You're right, but it's not as convenient.

2. **Bassam:**   So you're going to the rock concert too?

   Lilia: I sure am. Would you hand me that map, please?

   Bassam: You mean this bus map? Are you taking the bus?

   Lilia: Yes, I am. How are you getting there?

   Bassam: I think I'll take the train. It's a lot faster.

   Lilia: Yes, but the bus is cheaper.

   Bassam: It's not that much cheaper.

   Lilia: Well, then, would you show me the train route?

   Bassam: Sure. It's easy. If you like, you can go with me.

   Lilia: Could I? I'd love to!

Answers to Sound Bites

Answers will vary. Here are the pros and cons discussed in the listening script:

	pro	**con**
car	convenient	expensive
bus	costs less	sometimes late
train	faster	

Activity Masters

Activity Master 7-1 can be assigned after students have completed Student Book page 79.

Spotlight on Present Continuous

Preparation

1. Introduce the concept of using the present continuous to describe action happening now by writing two or three example sentences on the board such as the following:

   - I am writing sentences on the board now.
   - You are reading the sentences on the board now.

2. To check comprehension of *now*, you can ask, "What time is it now?" Emphasize *now* by writing the time and date above the sentences on the board.

3. Introduce the use of present continuous to describe actions that are happening *soon* by writing additional sentences on the board, such as the following:

   - The class is taking a break at _____ (time).
   - We are going home at _____ (time) today.
   - We are starting class at _____ (time) tomorrow.

4. Write *soon* above these sentences.

5. Practice the concepts of *now* and *soon* further by providing more statements with the present continuous. Have learners respond with *now* or *soon* to identify when the action is happening. Here are some example sentences:

   - I'm having a party on Saturday.
   - You are listening to my sentences.
   - We are coming to school tomorrow.
   - The students are sitting in their chairs.

Presentation

1. Read the Spotlight on Present Continuous box with the class. Have learners repeat the sentences after you.

2. On the board write "I am studying English," along with the rest of the subject pronouns off to the side. Ask volunteers to write new sentences with other pronouns on the board. Explain any endings that students seem to have trouble with.

3. Demonstrate the contractions by erasing the *be* verb in the first conjugation and replacing it with the appropriate contraction. "I'm studying English." Ask students to contract the other sentences.

4. Present the negative form of present continuous by changing the word *English* in the sentences on the board to another language or course title and changing the first sentence to the negative sentence, "I'm not studying math." Again, ask volunteers to write the appropriate negative form on the board for each of the rest of the sentences.

Exercise 2

Presentation

Practice the questions orally with the class before having the students write the answers. Ask questions like these.

- José, are you looking for a job?
- Class, is José looking for a job?
- Maria, are you taking the bus home from school today?
- Class, is Maria taking the bus home from school today?

Extension

1. For additional speaking practice have students make a grid to interview class-mates using the questions under the Spotlight Box. Put the following example on the board for the students to copy:

	Name	yes	no
Are you looking for a job now?			
Are you taking the bus home after school today?			
Are you walking home after class today?			
Are you staying home this weekend?			

2. Demonstrate the interview and writing techniques for this exercise by choosing a learner or learners to practice for the class. Write *yes* or *no* as the volunteers respond to the questions.

3. Have the learners walk around the class to interview classmates. Then ask them to report the information to the class or to a partner. Here are some possible reports:

   - Binh is looking for a job. He isn't taking the bus home from school today. He is walking home. He is staying home this weekend.

   - Maria isn't looking for a job. She is taking the bus home from school today. She isn't walking home. She isn't staying home this weekend.

4. For additional writing practice have learners write sentences about the information they collected in the interviews.

Answers to Exercise 2

Answers will vary. Here are some possible answers:
1. No, I'm not. I'm not looking for a job now.

2. Yes, I am. I'm taking the bus home from school today.

3. No, I'm not. I'm not walking home after class today.

4. Yes, I am. I'm staying home this weekend.

Extension

Option 1: Have lower-level students memorize one of the Person to Person conversations and present it to the class.

Option 2: Pair a more advanced learner with a less advanced learner and have them work together to prepare and present a conversation.

Option 3: For further practice have more advanced learners work with partners to create additional conversations based on the conversations in Person to Person. Have them present the conversations to the class without using books or papers.

Workbook

Workbook page 39 can be assigned after students have completed Student Book page 80.

Activity Masters

Activity Master 7-2 can be assigned after students have completed Student Book page 80.

Spotlight on *Could* and *Would* for Requests

Preparation

1. Demonstrate the meaning of the words *could* and *would* by using them in sentences to make requests of individual students, as in the following examples:

   - Martin, could you help me for a minute? Would you erase the board for me please?
   - Maria, would you close the door, please?
   - Binh, would you please give this paper to José?

2. Repeat the requests as necessary until students understand and perform the task.

Presentation

1. Have volunteers read the questions and answers in the Spotlight Box aloud. Model pronunciation if needed.

2. Write the words *could* and *would* on the board. Suggest topics or problems and have the class help you make requests. Write the sentences on the board, or request a student to do it for you. Here are some examples.

   - I'm cold. The window is open. What request do I make? (Could you close the window, please?)
   - My car isn't working. I need a ride to class tomorrow. What request do I make? (Could you give me a ride to school tomorrow?)
   - I'm studying English at home. The music on the radio is loud. What request do I make? (Would you turn down the radio, please?}
   - I have a dollar. I need change to make a phone call. What request do I make? (Could you give me change for a dollar?)

3. Have learners work with partners to practice the requests on the board and give appropriate polite answers.

Extension

Option 1: Have less advanced students prepare a conversation using one of the requests written on the board and present it to the class.

Option 2: Have learners work in pairs to create four additional requests and answers. Have pairs present their conversations to the class without using books or papers.

Exercise 3

Presentation

1. Read the conversation and have the learners repeat after you. Ask students to identify any new or difficult words in the conversation. Explain them.

2. After students have completed the exercise with their partners, check comprehension by asking questions or having the learners prepare questions about the conversation. Here are some possible questions.

   - What problem does Bassam have?
   - Who is he calling?
   - What is the name of the towing company?
   - What is Bassam's location?
   - How long will he have to wait?

Answers to Exercise 3

1. Could / Would
2. Could / Would
3. please
4. Could / Would
5. please

Workbook

Workbook page 40 can be assigned after students have completed Student Book page 81.

Page 82

Get Graphic

Preparation

Make a transparency of the train schedule or copy a few lines of it on the board. Ask questions about the schedule. Point to the correct answers if students have trouble finding the information. Here are some sample questions:

- What time does the first train arrive in San Clemente? (5:11)
- What time will that train arrive at Union Station in Los Angeles? (6:36)

Answers to Get Graphic

1. 7:29   2. 8:38   3. 1 hour, 9 minutes   4. 6:01

Your Turn

Preparation

Give students an example to follow by choosing a destination and writing the answers to the questions on the board.

Page 83

Issues and Answers

Preparation

1. If necessary, explain that *being in favor of* means "thinking something is good, or good to do." Provide some examples. Then ask learners to suggest additional examples. Here are some possible sentences:
   - I am in favor of having longer weekends in the summer.
   - I am in favor of paying lower taxes.
   - I am in favor of cheaper public transportation.
2. Have learners study Issues and Answers in a group. Ask them to make a list of any words they don't understand. Explain the difficult words or ask other learners to provide definitions.

Wrap-Up

Presentation

Have students report the information on their T-charts. With the class decide which advantages and disadvantages are the most important. Make a class T-chart on the board. Have students write sentences under *Advantages* or *Disadvantages,* as appropriate.

Workbook

Workbook pages 41 and 42 can be assigned after students have completed Student Book page 84.

ANSWERS FOR PROGRESS CHECKS

Progress Check A

Speak or Write

1. He is waiting for the bus.

2. It comes every hour on the hour.

3. It's coming in 45 minutes.

4. He hates waiting for buses.

Listening Script

(Answers are underlined.)

Bassam (1) is <u>taking</u> the bus to work today. He has to (2) <u>wait</u> a long time for the next (3) <u>bus</u>. He (4) <u>needs</u> to have (5) <u>exact</u> (6) <u>change</u>, and he needs to ask the bus driver for a (7) <u>transfer</u>.

Bassam has his learner's (8) <u>permit</u>, and he is practicing for his (9) <u>driving</u> test. He is (1) <u>saving</u> money to buy a (10) <u>used</u> car. He also has to pay for (11) <u>insurance</u> and registration. A car is a big responsibility.

Progress Check B

Language Structures

1. is taking	2. is going	3. are leaving
4. are meeting	5. are not eating	6. are having

Content

1. T	2. F	3. F	4. T	5. F	6. T	7. T

ANSWERS TO ACTIVITY MASTERS

Activity Master 7-1

Answers will vary. Students will write classmates' names in front of the sentences.

Activity Master 7-2

1. 7:20 A.M.   2. 5 minutes   3. 6:00   4. 8:30   5. 8:30   6. 40 minutes

WORKBOOK ANSWERS

Practice 1

Answers will vary. Here are some possible answers.

1. need to   2. cross street   3. need to   4. change

5. have to   6. bus stop   7. wait   8. need to

9. transfer   10. have to   11. Buses   12. have to

Practice 6

1. are you doing?   2. We are doing   3. Is Ashley doing

4. she is reading   5. are the others doing?   6. Are they watching

7. we are looking   8. Are you coming   9. we are coming

Practice 7

Answers will vary. Here are some possible answers.

1. Could   2. Could   3. Could   4. Would   5. Could

Practice 8

Answers will vary. Here are some possible answers:

a. First, she needs to learn English.

b. After that, she has to study the California Driver's Manual.

c. Then she has to pass a test and get a learner's permit.

d. Next, she needs to practice driving.

e. Later, she needs to buy a car.

f. Finally, she will be independent.

Name _____   Date _____

PROGRESS CHECK A

SPEAK OR WRITE

Look at the pictures from Unit 7. Use the questions below to talk or write about each picture.

Which bus are you waiting for?

Bus number 7.

Oh, it comes every hour on the hour. It's coming again in 45 minutes, at 12:00.

I hate waiting for buses! They're so slow!

Questions

1. What is Bassam waiting for?

2. How often does the bus come?

3. When is the bus coming again?

4. How does Bassam feel about waiting for buses?

LISTEN

Listen and write the missing words.

Bassam is (1) _____ the bus to work today. He has to (2)

_____ a long time for the next (3) _____.

He (4) _____ to have (5) _____ (6) _____,

and he needs to ask the bus driver for a (7) _____.

    Bassam has his learner's (8) _____, and he is practicing for

his (9) _____ test. He is (10) _____ money to

buy a (11) _____ car. He also has to pay for (12) _____

and registration. A car is a big responsibility.

Name _____ Date _____

PROGRESS CHECK B

LANGUAGE STRUCTURES

Write the verbs. Use present continuous.

1. Bassam _____ the train to the rock concert. (*take*)

2. Lilia _____ with him on the train. (*go*)

3. They _____ on the 6:00 train. (*leave*)

4. They _____ some friends at the ticket booth. (*meet*)

5. Bassam and Lilia _____ dinner on the train. (*not eat*)

6. They _____ dinner at a restaurant near the concert. (*have*)

CONTENT

Read the sentences. Put a check under *True* or *False*.

	True	False
1. A new car has a factory warranty.	_____	_____
2. The red lights on the rear end of a car are called stop lights.	_____	_____
3. When I need to change buses, I ask the driver for a transit center.	_____	_____
4. A car that has broken windows because of an accident is damaged.	_____	_____
5. The paper that says you can practice driving is a driver's license.	_____	_____
6. When you have an accident, you must show proof of insurance to the police officer.	_____	_____
7. The breath test checks for alcohol.	_____	_____

REPRODUCIBLE MASTER
UNIT 7   ACTIVITY MASTER 7-1

LET'S TALK ABOUT TRANSPORTATION

Walk around the classroom. Ask questions about transportation.
When a classmate answers yes to your question, write the name of
the student at the beginning of the sentence. Try to write a different
name before every sentence!

Example: _____ is taking the bus home from school today.

Ask, "Are you taking the bus home from school today?"

1. _____ is taking a bus or train home from school today.

2. _____ is walking home from school today.

3. _____ is driving home after class today.

4. _____ is riding home with someone after class today.

5. _____ is planning to buy a car someday.

6. _____ is saving money for a car.

7. _____ is planning to get a driver's license someday.

8. _____ is studying for the driver's test.

9. _____ is learning how to drive.

10. _____ is thinking about traveling to another city.

REPRODUCIBLE MASTER
UNIT 7

ACTIVITY MASTER 7-2

MORE READING FOR REAL

Read the bus schedule and answer the questions below.

Elm Street	Central Avenue	Union Street	Hanover Street	Orange Avenue
6:00	6:20	6:30	6:35	6:40
6:30	6:50	7:00	7:05	7:10
7:00	7:20	7:30	7:35	7:40
7:30	7:50	8:00	8:05	8:10
8:00	8:20	8:30	8:35	8:40
8:30	8:50	9:00	9:05	9:10
9:00	9:20	9:30	9:35	9:40

1. Bassam lives on Central Avenue. He takes the bus to work on Orange Avenue. He starts work at 8:00 A.M. What time does he need to get on the bus at Central Avenue?

2. Henry gets on the bus at Union Street. He takes the bus to his school on Hanover Street. How many minutes does it take him to get to school by bus?

3. What time in the morning does the first bus arrive at Elm Street?

4. Maria lives on Union Street. She has a 9:00 doctor's appointment on Orange Avenue. What time does she need to get on the bus at Union Street?

5. Samir lives on Central Avenue. He's going to visit his friend on Hanover Street. He gets on the bus at 8:20 A.M. What time will his bus arrive at the Hanover Street bus stop?

6. Lilia lives on Elm Street. She takes the bus to work on Orange Avenue. How much time does it take her to get to work by bus?

OVERVIEW

Objectives

Skills and Structures

Understand and talk about the library and other places in the community

Learn how to get a library card

Talk about freedoms in the United States

Read a bar graph

Talk about and solve problems

Use an idea map

Use *should* and *shouldn't*

Use *this that*, *these*, and *those*

SCANS Competencies

Select technology: Student Book, Scene 2, page 91; Student Book, Sound Bites, Scene 2, page 91; Teacher's Manual, Activity Master 8-1.

Apply technology to task: Student Book, Scene 2, page 91; Student Book, Sound Bites, Scene 2, page 91; Teacher's Manual, Activity Master 8-1.

Apply problem solving skills: Student Book, Sound Bites, Scene 1, page 86; Student Book, Your Turn, page 87; Student Book, Wrap-Up, page 96; Teacher's Manual, Scene 1, Preparation, page 134; Teacher's Manual, Activity Master 8-1.

Realia

A *No Smoking* sign and other samples of signs posted in the classroom, at the school, or in the community

A library card

Registration forms for a library card

Samples of library materials such as children's books, magazines, adult literacy books, videotapes, cassette tapes, newspapers, and so on.

A few blank envelopes

A few stamps

A reproduction of the U.S. Constitution or the Bill of Rights

A sample list of the 100 citizenship questions

ACTIVITY NOTES

Page 85

Scene 1

Preparation

1. Give learners this problem scenario. Define the word *advice*. Start learners generating vocabulary and using their prior knowledge. Tell the story that follows or write it on the board.

   "I have a friend who likes to learn new things and visit interesting places, but my friend doesn't have much money. Can you help me think of some ideas to help my friend?"

2. Write students' ideas on the board and assess their ability to give advice. Do any of the students use *should?* What vocabulary do they generate? Leave their ideas on the board.

3. Write the word *advice* on the board. Point to students' ideas and the word advice. Say, "Thank you for your ideas. Thank you for your advice. Maybe your advice will help my friend."

Presentation

1. Tell students that in Scene 1 a person has a problem and is asking for advice.

2. Ask questions about the pictures in Scene 1.

   • In the first picture Pedro says, "I don't have much money." Does that mean he has a lot of money or a little money?

   • In the second picture Steve tells Pedro he should "see the world." What does he mean? What does Pedro think he means? How do you know?

   • How can you "see the world" with a library card?

Extension

1. Ask students if the advice from Scene 1 is in their advice on the board. Compare the advice in the story with the advice on the board. Do students agree with Steve's advice?

2. Have pairs of students role-play the Scene for the class in one of several ways. Bring in props or costumes to make the activity more interesting.

Option 1: Students can perform the lines as written. You can assign pairs or let students choose their own partners.

Option 2: Students can make a simple substitution in some lines (inserting the places they would like to visit, for example).

Option 3: More advanced students can ad-lib a conversation on the topic treated in the Scene or imagine they are in a conversation with the characters in the Scene.

Page 86

Sound Bites

While You Listen

Preparation

1. Ask questions about using community resources. Here are some examples:

   • How many places in the community do you visit in one week?

   • Do your friends and family members go out in the community too?

   • Do you have friends or family members who stay home all the time?

2. Read the Sound Bites introduction with the class and then have students look at the other illustrations to predict answers.

Presentation

1. Tell students that they will hear a conversation about several of Pedro's relatives. Explain that you will play the tape three times and that they should try to listen for specific names and place names. Tell them that they do not have to write anything the first time they listen; they will write their answers when you play the tape the second time. When you play the tape the third time, they will check their answers.

2. Play the tape three times. When you play the tape the second time, students should mark their answers in their books. When you play the tape the third time, students should check their answers individually.

After You Listen

Presentation

1. Have students work in pairs to compare their answers. Circulate among the students and answer any questions they may have.

2. Go over the correct answers with the class.

3. If necessary, play the tape a fourth time to clarify any parts that students may have found difficult.

Extension

Using the chart on the board created from the previous Vocabulary Prompts activity, have volunteers add the names, places, and reasons from the Sound Bites exercise to the chart. The class dictates the information as the volunteers write. Monitor and correct but let the students lead the activity. Keep the chart on the board for the Your Turn activity.

Listening Script

1. My mother stays home too much. She sits and thinks. She worries about the problems in her country. She should enjoy the fresh air. I think she should take a walk.

2. My sister is pregnant. She works hard, and she's always tired. She should see her doctor for a medical checkup.

3. My little nephew plays video games all afternoon. He should exercise with other kids his age. He should climb and run and jump.

4. My 14-year-old niece is always talking on the phone. She shouldn't talk so much. She should read more. She should study in a quiet place.

5. My grandfather is lonely. All his friends are in Mexico. He sits and watches TV all day. He should find new friends. And he should learn to read and write English.

Answers for Sound Bites

1. park   2. clinic   3. playground   4. library   5. adult school

Page 87

Spotlight on *Should* and *Shouldn't*

Preparation

1. Review the meaning of *advice*. See page 134 of the Scene 1 Activity Notes for this unit. Tell students that the word *should* is often used for giving advice.

2. Have students find examples of *should* in the sentences from the Sound Bites activity and read the examples aloud.

Exercise I

Preparation

Have students review the Sound Bites activity to clarify what each family member should do.

Presentation

After students have written the exercise in their notebooks, ask volunteers to give advice for each family member.

Answers to Exercise I

1. should	2. should	3. shouldn't	4. should
5. shouldn't	6. should	7. shouldn't	8. should

Your Turn

Preparation

With the class, brainstorm as many community places as possible in three minutes. Then have students name the local equivalents of those places, and use them in the Your Turn activity.

Extension

1. Have volunteers write their sentences on the board. Assess learners' ability to use *should* by having the class help you check and correct the sentences on the board. Here are questions to ask to encourage student participation:

   • Is the sentence correct?

   • How can we change the sentence to make it correct?

2. For further practice add your own incorrect sentences to the board for students to correct.

Workbook

Workbook pages 43 and 44 can be assigned after students have completed Student Book page 87.

Page 88

Your Turn

Extension

To teach an interesting cultural point, discuss fines and penalties in your community for infractions such as littering and parking in a handicapped space. Compare the laws and penalties of the community with those of other countries. Students can use the sentence starters below. You may want to write them on the board.

   • In my native country, you shouldn't _____.

   • In my native country, it's OK to _____ , but not here.

   • In the United States, you shouldn't _____.

Reading for Real

Preparation

Hold up a sample library registration form and ask students to predict what information someone needs to fill it out. Then list their guesses on the board and discuss them.

Presentation

1. Ask students to name any new or difficult words from the reading. Define any words they do not understand.

2. Have a volunteer explain *proof of residence*.

Exercise 2

Presentation

Point out that the answers to 1–3 can be found in the reading, but that question 4 is asking for students' opinions.

Answers to Exercise 2

1. Pedro should write his name, address, telephone number, social security number, and native language. He should also sign his name.

2. No, he shouldn't.

3. He needs to show the librarian his ID card and an envelope with his name and address and a canceled stamp on it.

4. Answers will vary.

Culture Corner

Preparation

1. Show a copy of the Constitution or the Bill of Rights. Alternatively, on the board draw the outline of a document with the word *Constitution* at the top followed by the words *We the People* within the document.

2. Ask students pre-reading questions such as these:
   - What's the name of this document?
   - Is this document important?
   - What's in it?
   - Why did people write this document?
   - Do you know any stories about the beginnings of the United States as a country?

3. Have students help you tell about the beginnings of the United States. Ask if there are citizenship students in the class who can share their knowledge. Give a general overview. The aim here is a cultural literacy lesson about basic facts most Americans already know about this era of U.S. history.

Exercise 3

Presentation

Point out that questions 1–4 can be answered with information from the reading but that question 5 asks for students' opinions based on what they know about libraries.

Extension

1. Locate the list of 100 questions used for citizenship test preparation. See Contemporary Books *Citizenship Now, Entry into Citizenship* and *Getting Your Citizenship* for more information or a list of the 100 questions. Search for the questions related to what has already been discussed. Share the questions with the class and have students guess answers.

2. Use this information to do sentence dictations. Writing ability is tested in this way in one part of citizenship exams.

Answers to Exercise 3

1. It is "Freedom to Read" Week.

2. Go to free talks and book readings. People can listen and share.

3. Freedom of speech means that people can say what they want. Freedom of the press means that people can write and read what they want.

4. The First Amendment to the Constitution gives people in the United States these freedoms.

5. Libraries want freedom so people can borrow any book they want.

Page 91

Scene 2

Preparation

1. If necessary, familiarize yourself with the local public library. Learn about the policies and procedures for using the library.

2. Find out if the card catalog is on computer, microfilm or microfiche, or actual cards. (All use basically the same subject, title, and author cataloguing system.)

3. At the library ask questions to address specific needs and interests of your students. Find out what special materials, facilities, programs, and other offerings the library has. Ask whether the local public library has an adult-literacy section with adult-beginner reading books or whether another branch in the area has a larger selection.

   Also ask whether there are volunteers available to assist students, whether a field trip would be possible or whether a library staff person would be available to come to the school to talk about the library.

4. Check to see if the local library has access to the Internet. Ask whether there are special hours offered for training, or whether patrons need to make an appointment.

   Find out whether the librarians are willing to work with beginning English speakers. Finally, find out whether volunteers available to assist students, or whether the teacher should provide a volunteer.

5. Use the local library as a guide for how closely the Student Book vocabulary and explanations in this unit are followed. Whenever possible, point out where the information in the book is the same and where it is different from your own local library.

Presentation

1. Ask questions about Scene 2. Here are some examples:
   - What does Pedro want to know about in the first picture?
   - What does Pedro want to know about in the second picture?
2. Explain the difference between the two computers.

Extension

Option 1: Students can perform the lines as written. You can assign pairs or let students choose their own partners.

Option 2: Students can make a simple substitution in some lines (inserting other things in the library, for example).

Option 3: More advanced students can ad-lib a conversation on the topic treated in the Scene or imagine they are in a conversation with the characters in the Scene.

Page 91

Sound Bites

While You Listen

Presentation

1. Tell students that they will hear one conversation. Explain that you will play the tape three times and that they should try to listen for the words in the Vocabulary Prompts. Tell them that they do not have to write anything the first time they listen; they will check off their answers when you play the tape the second time. When you play the tape the third time, they will review their answers.
2. Play the tape three times. When you play the tape the second time, students should mark their answers in their books. When you play the tape the third time, students should review their answers individually.

After You Listen

Presentation

1. Have students work in pairs to compare their answers. Circulate among the students and answer any questions they may have.
2. Go over the correct answers with the class.
3. If necessary, play the tape a fourth time to clarify any parts that students may have found difficult.

Listening Script

Carlos:	I don't know many of the things in the library. What is this?
Ms. Chan:	This is the computerized catalog. It can help you find things.
Carlos:	And what's that computer?
Ms. Chan:	That's the Internet computer.
Carlos:	Wow! Are these videotapes?
Ms. Chan:	Yes, you can borrow these for three days.

Carlos:	And those over there?
Ms. Chan:	Those are cassette tapes that you can check out.
Carlos:	Good. Those books over there are for children, right?
Ms. Chan:	Yes. That section has children's books.
Carlos:	Do you have magazines and newspapers?
Ms. Chan:	Oh, yes, those are over there. Did you see these adult literacy books? These are for adults learning to read. They are also good for adults learning English.
Carlos:	I'm still learning English. Maybe I'll take some of these.

Answers to Sound Bites

There should be checks by all items except for *reference books* and *dictionaries.*

Activity Masters

Activity Master 8-1 can be assigned after students have completed Student Book page 91.

Preparation

This activity practices the SCANS competencies of selecting and applying technology to a task. In this activity, learners discuss technology in a library. Use this master either as a small group activity or as an active, kinesthetic, whole-class activity.

1. Before class make enough copies for every group to have one handout. For a whole-class activity probably no more than two copies will be needed. Next, cut the problems and solutions into separate slips. Make a set of problems and a set of solutions for each group. For the whole-class activity make enough slips to give one to every student in class. (Half the slips are problems, and half are solutions.)

2. Mix the order of slips and distribute them to groups or individuals. Groups work independently to match problems and solutions. For the whole-class activity, students circulate around the room searching for a match.

3. Review and check comprehension by having a representative of each group read the matched problems and solutions aloud to the class. Alternatively, for the whole-class activity, matched pairs can read their problems and solutions aloud to the class.

Page 92

Spotlight on Demonstrative Pronouns
This, That, These, and *Those*

Preparation

Use the items you collected for the Vocabulary Prompts to model demonstrative pronouns. For example, display the various items. Hold up a cassette tape and say, "This is a cassette tape." Then point to another item on the table and say, "That's a videotape," and so on. Elicit from students when to use *this, that, these* or *those.*

Exercise 4

Preparation

Have student pairs practice orally with materials around the room. Circulate, but try to allow student pairs to correct each other.

Answers to Exercise 4

1. This is a computer for the librarian.
2. This is an English dictionary.
3. Those are books for adults.
4. These are videotapes for adults.

Spotlight on the Demonstrative Adjectives *This, That, These,* and *Those*

Preparation

1. Dramatize the artwork in the Spotlight Box so students can see how the librarian is gesturing as she describes the sections of the library. Use the demonstrative adjectives from the Spotlight Box as you gesture.

2. Add examples to your dramatization to reinforce the use of demonstrative adjectives.

Answers to Exercise 5

1. This   2. That   3. These   4. Those

Workbook

Workbook pages 45 and 46 can be assigned after students have completed Student Book page 93.

Get Graphic

Preparation

Ask students to discuss the following questions in small groups:

- What does it mean to be a good reader? a poor reader?
- Are you a good reader or a poor reader? Why?

Exercise 6

Presentation

Be sure students understand they should fill in the blanks with dollar amounts from the graphic.

Answers to Exercise 6

1. $355   2. $910   3. $531   4. $709   5. $496

Your Turn

Presentation

When students have completed the sentence, ask how many of them think that this is a good title for this graphic.

Answers to Your Turn

This bar graph shows that *good readers* make more money than *poor readers*.

In Your Experience

Extension

1. Have groups share their answers with the class.

2. Have students form pairs to make Venn diagrams about the materials they read.

3. Each partner should label the outer section of one of the two overlapping circles with his or her name. Partners should discuss with each other what they read.

4. Inside the outer section of the student's circle, the student lists the reading materials he or she reads that his or her partner does not.

5. Partners should work together to list the reading materials used by both in the overlapping section of the two circles.

6. Display and discuss the Venn diagrams.

Activity Masters

Activity Master 8-2 can be assigned after students have completed Student Book page 95.

Preparation

1. Tell learners that there is another important reason to read. Reading aloud is the most important activity an adult can engage in to help a child learn to read. This is a good investment in the child's future. Research shows that being able to read well is the most important factor in school success.

2. Take a poll. How many learners are parents? grandparents? siblings of younger brothers and sisters? aunts? uncles? How many have friends or neighbors with young children? Emphasize that nonparents as well as parents can help children by reading to them.

3. This activity practices the SCANS competency of communicating information in the form of a pair dictation. Partners will dictate to each other. They will read and write tips on how to read to children. So that pairs can successfully complete the activity on their own, review clarification techniques from Unit 1, Culture Corner, page 6.

4. Before class make half as many copies as you have students. Cut the handouts in half and keep the halves separate.

Presentation

1. After pairing students, but before distributing handouts, have partners designate who is Person A and Person B. Distribute Person A handouts to the As and Person B handouts to the Bs.

2. Before pair work begins, have all the As sit together and all the Bs sit together to become "experts" of their half of the handout. In expert groups of three or four students together, they can read and discuss their tips. In the expert groups, learners can use each other and the teacher as a resource to check vocabulary meaning and practice pronunciation.

3. Learners can then return to their original partners to complete the activity.

Issues and Answers

Extension

Set aside time, if possible, for one or more of the following activities.

1. Librarian's Day. Invite a librarian to your class to talk about the library. Have learners ask some of the questions generated in the groups.

2. Go on a field trip to the library.

3. Have a library show and tell. Encourage students to go on their own or in pairs to visit the neighborhood library. Those that have gone can show the class what they borrowed from the library and tell about the experience and the resources.

Wrap-Up

Preparation

Refer to Scene 1 on page 85 and Sound Bites on page 86. Review places and reasons to use the community resources mentioned on page 86.

Extension

As a creative way to present the advice, have learners role-play giving their advice to Sue in person. You play Sue's role and always ask *why* after any suggestion. The groups will need to verbalize their reasons for their suggestions and persuade "Sue" to take their advice.

Workbook

Workbook pages 47 and 48 can be assigned after students have completed Student Book page 96.

ANSWERS FOR PROGRESS CHECKS

Progress Check A

Speak or Write

1. Pedro thinks his mother should take a walk in the park because she stays home and doesn't exercise. His grandfather should go to school to learn English and make friends. His sister should go to the clinic because she is pregnant. His nephew should go to the playground to play with other kids. His niece should go to the library because she should read more.

2. Answers will vary.

Listening Script

Julio and I are two students from Mr. Grant's Vocational English as a Second Language Laboratory, or VESL lab. We went to the library together. We were a little nervous. We didn't understand the library computers. We didn't know how to use the Internet. We asked the librarian to help us. She showed us how to use the Internet. In the library, we found a lot of books, newspapers, and magazines. We saw CDs and videos there too. Now we go to the library twice a week. We really enjoy it.

Listen

1. False   2. True   3. False   4. False   5. True   6. True

Progress Check B

Language Structures

1. These   2. That   3. This   4. Those   5. These

Content

1. community 2. card   3. borrow   4. magazine

5. ask   6. librarian 7. Internet

ANSWERS TO ACTIVITY MASTERS

Activity Master 8-1

I don't have a library card. / You should fill out a library registration form, show some ID, and bring proof of residence.

I want to read car magazines. / You should look at the magazine section of the library.

My kids want books. / You should go to the children's section of the library.

I can't use the Internet. / You should ask the librarian to help you.

I want to practice listening to English. / You should borrow some language tapes.

I don't read well. / You should borrow books from the adult literacy section.

My roommate is noisy, and I can't study. / You should go to the library because it is quiet.

I want books about Mexico. / You should look up Mexico on the computerized catalog.

I like to see movies, but I don't have much money. / You should borrow movie videotapes from the library.

I want to buy used books. / You should ask the librarian about book sales.

Activity Master 8-2

Tips for Adults Reading to Children

Person A: Sit and read to children of all ages, babies too.

Person B: Choose easy books and books you like.

Person A: Teach a child how to sit and hold a book.

Person B: Talk about the pictures. Guess what's on the next page.

Person A: Take care of library books. Teach children not to write in them and not to eat or drink when reading them.

Person B: If a child doesn't want to sit and read, try again later. Reading together should be fun.

WORKBOOK ANSWERS

Practice 1

1. should	2. should	3. should	4. should
5. shouldn't	6. should	7. should	

Practice 2

1. should 2. should walk in the park 3. should go to the dentist 4. should see a doctor
5. shouldn't watch TV 6. should talk to the librarian 7. should get a library card
8. should play on the playground 9. shouldn't smoke

Practice 4

1. This	2. that	3. This	4. those	5. These
6. those	7. those	8. that	9. These	10. this

Practice 5

1. 0   2. 0   3. all   4. yes

REPRODUCIBLE MASTER
UNIT 8

PROGRESS CHECK A

SPEAK OR WRITE

Look at the pictures from Unit 8. Use the questions below to talk or write about each picture.

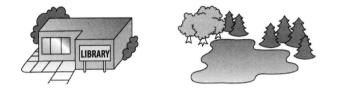

Questions

1. What places in the community does Pedro think his family should visit and why?

2. What places in the community do you like to visit and why?

LISTEN

While you listen, put a check under *True* or *False*.

	True	False
1. This story is about two librarians.	_____	_____
2. Two students went to the library.	_____	_____
3. The librarian was too busy to help.	_____	_____
4. Students shouldn't use the Internet.	_____	_____
5. They should look around the library.	_____	_____
6. They go back again and again.	_____	_____

Name _____ Date _____

LANGUAGE STRUCTURES

Look at the picture and complete the sentences with *this, that, these,* or *those.*

1. _____ two books on my side of the table are for me.

2. _____ is a video about Brazil.

3. _____ is my library card.

4. _____ magazines are for my boyfriend.

5. _____ cassette tapes are for me to practice my English.

CONTENT

Complete the paragraph with the words below.

> right   librarian   Internet   community   card   read
> ask   borrow   freedom   magazines

The public library is the place I use most in my (1) _____. I have a

library (2) _____ so I can (3) _____ cassette tapes, (4)_____

books and more. I (5) _____ the (6) _____ to help me when I

can't find something. I like to use the (7) _____ to find information

from all over the world.

Name _____   Date _____

SOLVE PROBLEMS WITH LIBRARY TECHNOLOGY AND RESOURCES

Match Problems and Solutions

Teacher Note: This handout should not be duplicated as a class set. Make only one copy and cut the problems and solutions into individual strips for group work or as a whole-class Reproducible. Keep this original as an answer key. See further instructions on page 141.

Problem	Solution
I don't have a library card.	You should fill out a library registration form, show some ID, and bring proof of residence.
I want to read car magazines.	You should look at the magazine section of the library.
My kids want books.	You should go to the children's section of the library.
I can't use the Internet.	You should ask the librarian to help you.
I want to practice listening to English.	You should borrow some language tapes.
I don't read well.	You should borrow books from the adult literacy section.
My roommate is noisy, and I can't study.	You should go to the library because it is quiet.
I want books about Mexico.	You should look up *Mexico* on the computerized catalog.
I like to see movies, but I don't have much money.	You should borrow movie videotapes from the library.
I want to buy used books.	You should ask the librarian about book sales.

ACTIVITY MASTER 8-2

Teacher Note: See page 143 for directions on this activity.

Person A

Tips for Adults Reading to Children

1. Sit and read to children of all ages, babies too.

2. _____

3. Teach a child how to sit and hold a book.

4. _____

5. Take care of library books. Teach children not to write in them and not to eat or drink when reading them.

6. _____

_____

✂ ┄┄

Person B

Tips for Adults Reading to Children

1. _____

2. Choose easy books and books you like.

3. _____

4. Talk about the pictures. Guess what's on the next page.

5. _____

_____

6. If a child doesn't want to sit and read, try again later. Reading together should be fun.

UNIT 9

OVERVIEW

Objectives

Skills and Structures

Talk about job interviews

Listen to conversations about jobs

Put together two sentences

Read about job tips

Read about a business person

Use *can* and *can't*

Understand a bar graph

Read about problems and solve them

Use an idea map

Use *must, must not* and *have to*

SCANS Competencies

Organize and maintain information: Student Book, Reading for Real, page 101; Teacher's Manual, Reading for Real, page 157; Teacher's Manual, Issues and Answers Extension Activity, page 164.

Sociability: Student Book, Reading for Real, page 101; Student Book, Issues and Answers, page 107; Teacher's Manual, Reading for Real Presentation Activity, page 157; Teacher's Manual, Issues and Answers Extension Activity, page 164.

Realia

Newspaper want ads

Blank job application

Clothing that could represent *appropriate* or *not appropriate* clothes for a job interview (for example, a tie, high heels, sandals, or a rock concert T-shirt)

Materials that provide information on past jobs (Samples you have from your own job history, such as old résumés, an old address book, or a duplicate of a completed job application, a file folder, a shoe box or other type of container used to store such material)

Cookies (tasty realia to introduce the Culture Corner reading about an American cookie business)

ACTIVITY NOTES

Page 97

Scene 1

Preparation

1. Write the words *job interview* on the board and ask students questions such as the following:

- What happens at a job interview?
- Who is there?
- What do interviewers say and do?

2. List students' ideas on the board and assess the students' prior knowledge and vocabulary usage.

3. Incorporate vocabulary from Scene 1 such as *boss, employees, computer,* and so on.

4. Show the newspaper want ads. Explain that Manolo looked for a job in the want ads and is now at the job interview in Scene 1.

Presentation

Ask questions such as the following:

- In the first two pictures, what does the boss need to find out?

- What does Manolo want to know in the third picture? Does he like the answer?

Extension

Compare what happened in Scene 1 with the learners' ideas listed on the board about what happens at a job interview.

Option: More advanced learners can write a continuation of the dialogue in the Scene. Then have them perform it in front of the class.

Page 98

Sound Bites

Before You Listen

Preparation

Pantomime the vocabulary in Chart 1. Draw pictures on the board if necessary. Have students guess what you're describing. Repeat the procedure with Chart 2.

Presentation

After students work in groups, review Chart 2 by asking students to give specific examples of each job policy. For example, to *take off an hour for lunch* means to stop work at noon, for example, eat, and then start work again at 1:00 P.M. Review words that students are having trouble with.

1. Check to see if students can aurally discriminate between *can* and *can't*. Write *can* [kan] and *can't* [kant] on the board. Include the phonetic equivalents if you wish.

2. Give students some sample sentences and point to the appropriate word as you speak. Here are some examples:

- I can drive a car, but I can't drive a motorcycle.

- I can speak Spanish, and I can speak English too.

- I can't speak Vietnamese.

3. Point out that in the middle of a sentence, *can* sounds very short, but *can't* is long. The letter *a* is easy to hear in the word *can't,* but the *t* is not. Therefore, listening for the *a* is more helpful than listening for the *t* when trying to hear if the word is *can* or *can't* in the middle of a sentence.

4. Put the number 1 over *can* and the number 2 over *can't*. Give a sentence with *can* or *can't* and have learners put up one finger or two depending on which word they hear. Ask them not to shout out answers but to use fingers so you can check the listening of all the students. They could also hold up 3 x 5 cards with *can* written on one side and *can't* written on the other.

5. On the board list pairs of sentences that are different only in that one sentence contains *can* and the other *can't.* Have learners practice the same exercise independently with partners while you circulate and check pronunciation and comprehension skills.

While You Listen

Presentation

1. Before playing the tape, tell students to listen especially for the difference between *can* and *can't* to fill out Chart 1.

2. Stop the tape after the first four conversations for Chart 1. Do the After You Listen activity.

3. Continue the tape so that students can complete Chart 2.

After You Listen

Preparation

Check students' comprehension of the jobs at the bottom of the page before asking them to match the person with the best job.

Listening Script

1. Human Resources Manager: Hello, Tony. Nice to meet you. I'm Jean Moseby, the Human Resources manager. First, why don't you tell me a bit about your skills?

   Tony: Well, I can repair cars pretty well. I can do landscaping, but I don't like it very much. And I can't work on weekends because I need to be with my family.

   Human Resources Manager: Can you type? We need someone who can type.

   Tony: No, I can't type, and I can't use a computer either.

2. Human Resources Manager: You're Lawanda Towns? Nice to meet you, Lawanda. I'm Jean Moseby, the Human Resources manager. Can you tell me a bit about your skills?

   Lawanda: I'm good with cars. I can repair foreign and domestic cars. I also have a license to drive a truck.

   Human Resources Manager: Can you work on weekends?

   Lawanda: Sure. It's OK with me to work on weekends.

3. Human Resources Manager: Hello, Siu. Nice to meet you. I'm Jean Moseby, the Human Resources manager. First, why don't you tell me a bit about your skills?

   Siu: Well, I can work very hard, and I like to work overtime too. I type 60 words per minute with no mistakes. I'm also good with computers. I can communicate well on the phone and in person, but I can't drive.

4. Human Resources Manager: You're Alfredo? Nice to meet you. I'm Jean Moseby, the Human Resources manager. First, can you tell me a bit about your skills?

   Alfredo: I'm strong, and I'm a good worker. I like to work in a warehouse because I can lift heavy loads. I can repair most machines, but I'm not good at repairing autos. I like to work early, and I can work long and hard.

5. Narrator: Alfredo is talking to a friend about work.

   Alfredo: What do you like about the job?

   Jack: Well, I can start early and leave early. If I start at 8:00, I can leave at 4:00.

   Alfredo: I like that idea.

   Jack: And here's another thing I like: I can take a personal day off each year. And I can take a whole hour for lunch.

   Alfredo: You do deliveries, right?

   Jack: That's right.

   Alfredo: Can you use the company car on weekends?

   Jack: No, I can't.

   Alfredo: Do they have any openings at your company?

   Jack: I don't know. Talk to Jean Moseby, the Human Resources manager.

Answers to Sound Bites

Chart 1

Tony: a check mark on *repair automobiles*

Lawanda: check marks on *repair automobiles, drive a truck*

Siu: check marks on *use a computer, type 60 words per minute*

Alfredo: a check mark on *lift heavy loads*

Chart 2

Start work early and leave early: yes

Take a personal day off: yes

Use the company car: no

Take off an hour for lunch: yes

Answers to After You Listen

1. Tony   2. Siu   3. Alfredo   4. Lawanda

Spotlight on Meanings of *Can* and *Can't*

Preparation

1. Look again at Charts 1 and 2 on the preceding page to match the charts with the use of *Can.* Chart 1 is *Abilities/Skills,* and Chart 2 is *Expressing Rules.*

2. Before the first notebook exercise, write a comprehensive list of the students' job skills on the board as they dictate them to you. Explain the skills to others when necessary. Add any skills that haven't been mentioned but that may apply.

3. Ask students if they can use a computer. When you get a negative answer, write it on the board as "I can't use a computer yet." Explain to students that job skills should be listed as positively as possible. Using *yet* in negative sentences lets interviewers know that you are willing to learn.

Exercise 1

Preparation

To practice stating job skills, ask students questions using the job skills listed on the board for the Spotlight. Model the appropriate language. For example, say, "Oh, you can speak Spanish," or "Oh, then you can type," or "So you can't use a computer yet." Students can refer to the list on the board as they work independently.

Answers to Exercise 1

Answers will vary but should be personal and in complete sentences.

Exercise 2

Presentation

When groups have finished listing their rules, have the class choose the five best rules. Place them on a wall in the classroom.

Person to Person

Extension

Option 1: Have pairs ask each other the questions in Person to Person and answer according to their own skills.

Option 2: More advanced student pairs can interview each other using their own questions about job skills.

Workbook

Workbook page 49 can be assigned after students have completed Student Book page 99.

Spotlight on Compound Sentences with
and. . . too and *and . . . either*

Preparation

1. Ask a volunteer to write two job skills on the board. Then ask the class about that person's job skills. For example, ask, "Can Chu-Yen use a computer? Can he speak English?" Tell students that the two positive sentences can be combined into one sentence. Then write the sentence on the board and emphasize where *and* and *too* are placed. Repeat the process with another student and leave the sentences on the board.

2. Ask a third student to come to the board and write two job skills that he or she doesn't have. Then ask the class about the student's job skills. "Can Helena type? Can she speak Chinese?" Tell students that the two negative sentences can be combined into one sentence. Then write the sentence on the board and emphasize where *and* and *either* are placed.

Extension

To reinforce the idea that *and. . . too* and *and. . . either* are used to combine two sentences that are both positive or both negative, ask students to break the compound sentence examples in the Spotlight Box into separate simple sentences. Have them check their sentences with a partner.

Answers to Exercise 3

1. Lawanda can drive a car, and she can drive a truck too.
2. Alfredo is strong, and he is a hard worker too.
3. Tony can't type well, and he can't communicate well with others either.
4. Nora and Joseph don't have a computer, and they don't have a typewriter either.
5. Mohammed can come to work early, and he can leave early too.
6. Komiko doesn't take an hour for lunch, and she doesn't leave the office either.

Exercise 4

Preparation

1. Give students a quick comprehension check before they find partners. Ask them to combine the following statements in their notebooks:

   • I can speak English. I can use a computer.
   • I can't speak French. I can't type very fast.

2. Elicit the correct answers and write them on the board for students to refer to.

Workbook

Workbook page 50 can be assigned after students have completed Student Book page 100.

Activity Masters

Activity Master 9-1 can be assigned after students have completed page 100.

Preparation

1. Create an overhead transparency of the activity or write the questions on the board. Read through the questions before distributing the handouts.

2. For any new vocabulary give examples. For example, to explain the skill *follow directions,* say, "Please write the date on the board and then give me the chalk." Wait for a volunteer to do so and congratulate the person for being able to follow directions.

3. Use the transparency or the questions on the board to interview one student. Begin by asking the questions yourself, but after the first few have students do the asking while you write the person's responses.

Presentation

Distribute papers and have learners move around the class to find three other learners to interview. Another strategy is to have learners work in groups of four, in which each learner interviews the three others in the group.

Extension

1. Role-play a job interview. Focus on asking about job skills but ask other appropriate questions as well. Students can practice in pairs, and then volunteers can perform their conversation for the class.

2. Using the answers collected from the Activity Master, students can give a summary, in front of the class, of another student's job skills. In their summary, they can use *can* and *can't.* This is also good review practice to help students to distinguish between *can* and *can't.*

Page 101

Reading for Real

Presentation

1. Have students read silently before reviewing with a partner and with the class.

2. Address the SCANS competency of sociability by analyzing and practicing the "American" handshake, eye contact, facial expressions, and other cultural tips presented in this reading. Students need these social skills to make a positive first impression at the interview.

3. Demonstrate a firm handshake by testing students' handshakes and assess whether they are too firm or too limp. Explain to students the subtle implications. For example, if you give a limp handshake, people may think that you don't like them or that you are a weak person. If you squeeze too hard, people may think you are aggressive.

Talk About It

Preparation

1. To prepare students to choose key words, write the following paragraph on the board or on a transparency:

"When you are writing a résumé, there are several things you need to remember. Always type your résumé on a typewriter or word processor. Never write it by hand. Center your name, address and phone number at the top of the page. Begin with a statement of what you would like to do, called an objective. Next, list your education, starting with the most recent school you attended. Generally, you don't have to go back any further than high school. Then list your previous jobs, again starting with the most recent. Be sure to write one or two phrases about what you did at each job. Finally, write *References available upon request* at the bottom of the page."

2. Give small groups about 10 minutes to read and find the key words in the paragraph. Have them share their lists with the class. Combine the lists into one class list and explain why these are the key words.

Extension

1. Bring in a box, a file folder, or another container that can be used for storing records related to past jobs. For convenience you can bring in your own records of your job history. Don't open the container yet.

2. Show a blank application. Explain that what is in the container helps you fill out job applications and prepares you for job interviews.

3. Have students guess what's inside before you open it.

4. Open the container and share with the class at least some of the following: old résumés, old completed job applications, old address books, old letterhead, business cards from previous jobs, and school records.

5. Share your own method or another possible method of organizing and maintaining job history information. Show, for example, that one folder is labeled *school records*, and another *résumés*.

6. Have learners share with a partner the ways they have organized and maintained job information or the ways they plan to organize and maintain it.

7. Focus also on helping learners be honest and positive (the last tip in the reading). Explain that positive talk about yourself is expected at a job interview in American culture. Learners need practice in saying good things about themselves and adding positive words to negative responses to interview questions. List vocabulary and expressions on the board to help students be honest and positive. For example, learners can respond with *not yet* or *a little* instead of saying only *no* when answering a question.

Page 102

Culture Corner

Preparation

1. Bring in some cookies to share. Have groups discuss questions such as the ones below about food preferences and business ideas.
   - Do you like cookies?
   - Do your children like cookies?
   - Do Americans like cookies?
   - Are cookies popular in your country?
   - What foods are popular in your country?
   - What other food products would make a successful business in your native country or in the United States?

2. Have groups share their responses with the class.

Presentation

Have pairs of students read the story to help each other with any unfamiliar vocabulary. When students have finished the story, ask them to name any difficult words they would like you to define.

Answers to Exercise 5

1. a 2. a 3. a 4. b 5. b

Your Turn

Preparation

Tell students they are going to open their own business making cookies. Ask groups to make a list of things they need to know about to make their business successful. Have volunteers share their lists with the class.

Answers to Your Turn

Answers will vary. Possible answers include the following:

Debbi learned time management, people management and caring for others.

The things someone opening a business should know include the following: costs and money management, planning, what customers want.

Page 103

Scene 2

Preparation

On the board, write the terms *deadline, due date,* and *past due.* Give examples such as due dates on telephone bills or deadlines for paying rent.

Presentation

Explain that in Scene 2 Manolo has a deadline. Ask learners to answer questions such as the following while looking at the Scene 2 comic strip:

- When is the deadline? (Monday)
- What is Manolo's problem with this deadline? (He doesn't have money to buy clothes for the interview until Tuesday.)
- What does Manolo do to solve his problem?

Extension

Option 1: In small groups have students think of other ways Manolo could solve his problem. Write their ideas on the board.

Option 2: More advanced students can write a continuation of the dialogue between Manolo and Paco in their notebooks.

Sound Bites

Before You Listen

Preparation

Write the sentences below (minus the answers) on the board to help groups talk about the list at the bottom of the page. Have groups match each sentence on the board sentence with the appropriate example from the list.

- Here are three names, addresses, and phone numbers of people I know. (give references)
- Can I use your name on my application? (find people to recommend him)
- I'm here at the clinic because my new boss sent me. (take a drug test)
- Please fill out your name and social security number on this W-2 form before you start work. (fill out paycheck forms)

While You Listen

Preparation

Elicit from students the idea that the important thing for them to listen for is the deadline that Manolo has for doing the things on the list.

After You Listen

Presentation

After groups have checked their answers, provide the correct answers to the class. Explain any that students do not understand. You may wish to play the tape again to clarify the answers.

Listening Script

Human Resources Manager:	Well, we would like to give you a job, but we need to check references. You didn't put any references on your application.
Manolo:	References? You mean names of people I know?
Human Resources Manager:	People who can recommend you. All applicants must provide three references.
Manolo:	Well, my brother Paco and my father can recommend me. That's two. And—
Human Resources Manager:	No, the references must not be relatives. You have to give us names of other people.
Manolo:	Other people? Do they have to be people at companies? I don't know any. This is my first job in the United States.
Human Resources Manager:	They don't have to be employers, but they must not be relatives. You can ask friends if you want. But they should all have jobs. And you must give us their phone numbers and addresses.
Manolo:	OK, then. When do I have to do that?

Human Resources Manager:	By Monday. We have to make our choices by next week.
Manolo:	All right. What else do I have to do?
Human Resources Manager:	You need to take a drug test. All employees must be drug free.
Manolo:	When do I have to do that?
Human Resources Manager:	The results must be in by Monday. But you should do it this week. Do it today or tomorrow if you can. Here's the address of the test center.
Manolo:	All right, I'll go there today. Do I have to do anything else?
Human Resources Manager:	You'll have to fill out some forms for your paycheck, but you can do that later. We'll call you after the results of your test.
Manolo:	OK. Thank you.
Human Resources Manager:	Thank you.

Answers to Sound Bites

All items should be checked except for "fill out paycheck forms," which Manolo can do later.

Page 104

Spotlight on *Must* and *Must Not*

Preparation

1. Explain the term *express obligation*. For example, say, "It means to say that something is necessary to do."

2. On the board under the heading *Do,* write three rules students know they need to follow at school. For example, write, "Be on time. Do your homework. Speak English in class."

3. Explain to students that rules they need to follow often use *must*. On the board beside the first rule, write," You must be on time." Ask for volunteers to write sentences with must on the board for the next two rules.

4. Repeat the procedure for *must not.* On the board write negative rules under the heading *Don't.*

Exercise 6

Preparation

Have pairs of students review the form for any new or difficult words. Provide definitions if needed.

Answers to Exercise 6

| Drugs: | 1. must | 2. must | 3. must not | |
| Hours: | 1. must | 2. must not | 3. must not | 4. must |

Person to Person

Preparation

Have students in small groups list various occupations that interest them. Then with the class, list the occupations and one or two things students must do or have in order to do that job. Leave the lists on the board for students to refer to when they change the Person to Person conversation.

Workbook

Workbook page 51 can be assigned after students have completed Student Book page 104.

Page 105

Spotlight on *Must* and *Have to*

Refer to the general instructions on page xv in the Introduction.

Presentation

1. Emphasize that *must* and *have to* have the same meaning but that *must not* and *don't have to* have different meanings.

2. Put pairs of school-related sentences—one sentence with *must not* and the same sentence with *don't have to*—on the board. Have learners work with a partner to discuss and select the sentence with the more appropriate meaning. Check with the whole class to make sure all agree. Here are some sample contrasting sentences:

   • You don't have to bring a dictionary to class. You must not bring a dictionary to class.

   • You don't have to smoke in the classroom. You must not smoke in the classroom.

Exercise 7

Presentation

Have a volunteer read the directions aloud. Emphasize that students have two choices for each blank and that they should only use *must not / don't have to* when they see (*not*).

Answers to Exercise 7

1. must	2. Do, have to	3. must	4. must
6. don't have to	7. Do, have to		

Workbook

Workbook page 52 can be assigned after students have completed Student Book page 105.

Activity Masters

Activity Master 9-2 can be assigned after students have completed page 105. It should be completed in preparation for Get Graphic on page 106.

Preparation

Before having groups work independently, read the information and discuss abbreviations and new vocabulary as a whole group.

Presentation

1. Students may choose to draw a line from the ad to the best person for the job or list answers on a separate paper.
2. This is a good opportunity for collaborative learning, with group members taking the roles of leader, secretary, and reporter. (See Unit 4, Scene 1, Activity Notes, page 64 for further explanation.)

Page 106

Get Graphic

Preparation

1. Show a page of newspaper want ads.
2. Divide the class into groups of three. Give each group a different want ad, for a different kind of job, but make sure the ones you choose have specific qualifications listed. Ask students to read their ads and share the qualifications for each job with the class. Define any vocabulary needed. Leave the list of qualifications on the board for the Your Turn activity.

Exercise 8

Preparation

Point out that 70 percent of the employers surveyed wanted their employees to have a good attitude. Ask students, "What does it mean to have a good attitude at work in the United States? What does it mean in your native country?"

Answers to Exercise 8

1. a
2. a. 33%   b. 8%   c. 37%   d. 70%
3. a. 3   b. 4   c. 2   d. 1

Your Turn

Preparation

1. On the board list jobs that learners are interested in. Add synonyms and related jobs. Group similar jobs together.
2. Regroup students by like interests. Distribute newspaper want ads. Have each group specialize in researching only the jobs that interest the group.

Issues and Answers

Preparation

1. In small groups have students think about their own work situations. How did they feel when they interviewed for their first job? How did they present their job skills and experience? If students have never worked, have them say how they will feel and what they will do when they interview.

2. Ask for a student volunteer who has a job to tell the class about an incident when he or she had problems with the boss. You may wish to choose a more advanced student and clear this with the student ahead of time to avoid embarrassment.

Extension

1. Have groups work together to list ideas about how to create a file on past, present, and future volunteer work opportunities.

2. Have learners use the questions in Abdul's response to *No Experience* to interview each other about their volunteer work.

3. Learners with no formal job experience need to practice talking about their job skills, including any volunteer experience they may have.

Wrap-Up

Preparation

Have groups search the unit for job interview questions.

Presentation

To encourage meaningful interaction, before students change groups, have each group decide the job policies of the group "company" and the specific job skills they are looking for in a job applicant. After students change groups, have the groups determine the best applicant for the job and share their reasons with the class.

Workbook

Workbook pages 53 and 54 can be assigned after students have completed Student Book page 108.

ANSWERS FOR PROGRESS CHECKS

Progress Check A

Speak or Write

1. They are talking because it is a job interview. The manager is interviewing Manolo and asking about his job skills.

2. Manolo can use a computer, and he can operate a cash register.

3. Manolo wants to know if he can start early and leave early.

4. Answers will vary. Here is a possible answer:

    Yes, this is important because Manolo needs to be home at 5:30 to take care of his children.

Listening Script

Hien Pham has an interesting job. Hien is a volunteer teacher. He doesn't get paid. He teaches people to speak and write in Vietnamese.

Hien has many good job skills. He can speak Vietnamese, and he can speak English too. He can communicate well in two languages. He can work well with people.

He can't work week nights because he goes to night class Monday through Thursday to learn more English. In the future, Hien wants to be an English teacher, and he wants to study computers. He wants a job that uses all his job skills.

Listen

1. True   2. False   3. True   4. False   5. True

Progress Check B

Language Structures

1. Lawanda can drive a car, and she can drive a truck too.
2. Alfredo can't speak French, and he can't understand French either.
3. Paula can read English, and she can write English too.
4. Mary can't work evenings, and she can't work weekends either.
5. Blong can use computers, and he can fix computers too.

Content

1. tips   2. references
3. skills   4. interview
5. family   6. appropriate
7. firm   8. honest

ANSWERS TO ACTIVITY MASTERS

Activity Master 9-1

Answers will vary.

Activity Master 9-2

Answers will vary. Here are some possible answers.

Childcare job—Mary

Computer job—Shukri

Construction job—Paula

Cook—Ignacio

Extra person—Blong. Possible job: truck driver or repair person.

REPRODUCIBLE MASTER
Unit 9

WORKBOOK ANSWERS

Practice 1

1. can't 2. can 3. can't 4. can 5. can 6. can't

Practice 2

1. Siu can use a calculator, and he can repair computers too.

2. Tony can't use a calculator, and he can't work evenings either.

3. Alfredo can work evenings, and he can landscape too.

4. Thuy can landscape, and she can repair computers too.

5. Paul can't use a calculator, and he can't work evenings either.

Practice 3

1. must 2. must 3. must not 4. must 5. must 6. must not

Practice 4

1. must 2. must 3. must not 4. must 5. must not

Practice 5

1. doesn't have to 2. must not 3. must not 4. must
5. doesn't have to 6. must not 7. doesn't have to 8. must

Practice 6

1. Yes, he does.

2. Yes, he did.

3. No, he wasn't.

4. Yes, he was.

5. Yes, he does.

6. Yes, he does.

© NTC/Contemporary Publishing Group, Inc.

REPRODUCIBLE MASTER
UNIT 9

PROGRESS CHECK A

SPEAK OR WRITE

Look at the pictures from Unit 9. Use the questions below to talk or write about each picture.

Questions

1. In the first picture why are Manolo and the manager talking?

2. What are some of Manolo's job skills?

3. In the second picture what does Manolo want to know?

4. Is this important? Why?

LISTEN

While you listen, put a check under *True* or *False*.

	True	False
1. Hien is a volunteer teacher.	_____	_____
2. He gets paid.	_____	_____
3. He has many job skills.	_____	_____
4. He can't speak English.	_____	_____
5. He is a teacher and a student.	_____	_____

Name _____ Date _____

UNIT 9   PROGRESS CHECK B

LANGUAGE STRUCTURES

Write compound sentences about these students' job skills.
Use *can* or *can't*.

1. (drive a car, drive a truck: yes) Lawanda _____

   _____

2. (speak French, understand French: no) Alfredo _____

   _____

3. (read English, write English: yes) Paula _____

   _____

4. (work evenings, work weekends: no) Mary _____

   _____

5. (use computers, fix computers: yes) Blong _____

   _____

CONTENT

Write the missing words. Use the words below.

family   skills   references   honest
appropriate   tips   firm   interview

Here are some important (1) _____ about finding a

job. Sometimes you must list names of (2) _____ on

your job application. It's a good idea to practice talking about your

job (3) _____ before a job (4) _____.

If you don't have much job experience, remember that Debbi Fields

learned a lot about business through her (5) _____.

At the interview wear (6) _____ clothes. Smile. Give a

(7) _____ handshake. You must not lie but always be

(8) _____.

Name _____ Date _____

JOB SKILLS INTERVIEW

Interview three classmates. Ask all the questions for each interview. Write the student's name at the top of the column. Write *Yes* or *No* for each question. Put a check by all the yes answers.

Questions	Student 1	Student 2	Student 3
1. Can you speak two languages?	_____	_____	_____
2. Can you communicate in English?	_____	_____	_____
3. Can you use a computer?	_____	_____	_____
4. Can you work well with others?	_____	_____	_____
5. Can you drive?	_____	_____	_____
6. Can you repair cars?	_____	_____	_____
7. Can you cook?	_____	_____	_____
8. Can you take care of children?	_____	_____	_____
9. Can you lift heavy loads?	_____	_____	_____
10. Can you fix things?	_____	_____	_____
11. Can you follow directions?	_____	_____	_____
12. Can you learn new things easily?	_____	_____	_____

UNIT 9   ACTIVITY MASTER 9-2

MORE READING FOR REAL: WANT ADS

In a small group read the four ads. Then read about the five people looking for jobs. Discuss the jobs and the job skills. Match each job with the best person for the job. Write the name of a job for the extra person.

Childcare Downtown daycare center needs P/T help. Exp., likes children. $5.60/hr. 697-6943	Blong—He can repair things. He can drive a truck. He can't communicate well.
Computers Sales help in customer service. Exp. in trouble-shooting and repair of computers a plus. 555-6875	Ignacio—He can lift heavy loads. He can cook. He can do yard work. He can't work evenings.
Construction Shop helper, reliable, must be 18 yrs., F/T, 555-3453	Mary—She can type and use computers. She can cook. She can baby-sit. She can't work full-time.
Cook F/T, all shifts, exp., good communication skills, 012-6754	Paula—She can communicate well. She can use construction tools. She can't cook.
Possible job for the extra person:	Shukri—She can use computers. She can work on weekends. She can't drive.

OVERVIEW

Objectives

Skills and Structures

Talk about people's problems

Learn about finding bargains

Read ads

Understand a time line

Read about coupons

Use a time line

Use indirect objects

Use comparative adjectives

Use *could* and *couldn't*

SCANS Competencies

Allocate money: Student Book, Wrap-Up, page 120; Student Workbook, Budget Time line, page 60; Teacher's Manual, Activity Master 10-2.

Participate as a member of a team: Student Book, Reading for Real/Your Turn, page 113; Student Book, Culture Corner/In Your Experience, page 114; Student Book, Get Graphic/In Your Experience, page 118; Teacher's Manual, Culture Corner Extension Activity, page 176; Teacher's Manual, Activity Master 10-2.

Realia

Shopping ads

Shopping coupons

Two newspaper ads for the same product

Newspapers, one for each group

An ad for a fax machine

A credit card

An application for a credit card

A paper bag

ACTIVITY NOTES

Page 109

Scene 1

Preparation

1. On the board draw a picture of a table with a *for sale* sign on it. The learners are the customers, and the teacher is the salesperson. Ask students, "Do you want to buy my table? It's a real bargain—a good table at a good price."

2. Add details to show that the table is a bargain. For example, when a learner asks about the price, you can respond, "It's only $5.00!" Write the price on the board and say, "It's a real bargain." Write the word *bargain* on the board.

3. Conclude the activity with a final sale and payment discussion. For example, say something such as the following: "I see you have a credit card. I'm sorry, I don't accept checks or credit cards. Cash only, please."

4. Ask students how many of them use checks and credit cards, and ask them to explain why or why not.

5. Ask, "Where can a person find a table for $5.00?" List responses on the board. See whether learners generate the vocabulary from the unit, such as shopping at *yard sales, second-hand stores,* and *flea markets.* (Note: the names for some of these various kinds of shopping venues change, in different regions of the country. *Flea market, swap meet,* and *open market* could all describe the same kind of situation. Choose the name that is most common in your area and use it throughout the unit.)

Presentation

1. Tell students that in Scene 1 someone is looking for a bargain.

2. Ask questions such as the following about Scene 1:

   • In the first picture why is Mei buying furniture?

   • She already bought a table and a lamp, How much money does she have left to buy a desk and chairs? Is this enough to buy the furniture she wants?

   • In the second picture where does Nicole say Mei should go? Why is Mei confused?

   • In the third picture what does Nicole think Mei will find at a yard sale?

Extension

Have pairs of students role-play the Scene for the class in one of several ways. Bring in props or costumes to make the activity more interesting.

Option 1: Students can perform the lines as written. You can assign pairs or let students choose their own partners.

Option 2: Students can make a simple substitution in some lines (inserting the places they would go to for bargains, for example).

Option 3: More advanced students can ad-lib a conversation on the topic treated in the Scene or imagine they are in a conversation with the characters in the Scene.

Page 110

Sound Bites

While You Listen

Preparation

1. Read the list of stores aloud.

2. Have students work in pairs to write in their notebooks which store they think each picture represents. Tell students to save their guesses until they have listened to the conversation on the tape.

Presentation

Tell students they will hear one conversation among four different people. Each has different opinions about what Mei should do.

After You Listen

Review the correct answers with the class. Ask students to look back in their notebooks at the guesses they made in the preparation activity. If any of the students guessed correctly, ask those students to share with the class what they saw in the pictures that gave them the answer.

Listening Script

Woman 1: Say, Mei, here's an idea for you. What about second-hand stores? They have good prices on used clothing and furniture. Sometimes you can get beautiful clothes very cheap.

Man 1: Or you could go to a yard sale. They have the best prices there. And there are sales every weekend. I'll look in my newspaper for you and get you some addresses.

Woman 2: But discount stores are better than yard sales. You can buy new products there. Also, discount stores can deliver things to you.

Man 2: I like factory outlets too. At a factory outlet a company sells its products to customers at a discount. You can buy high quality products there.

Woman 1: You can also use the want ads. People sell lots of things to other people through want ads in the newspaper. You can get some super bargains that way.

Man 1: And what about flea markets? People rent spaces and sell lots of different kinds of things. The prices are good too. Tell me when you want to go, and I'll take you to a great one.

Answers to Sound Bites

1. second-hand store   2. yard sale   3. discount store   4. factory outlet

5. want ads   6. flea market

Answers to After You Listen

Answers will vary. Here are some possible answers:

Mei should go to second-hand stores because they have good prices.

Maybe Mei doesn't have a truck. She should go to a discount store where the store can deliver.

Page 111

Spotlight on Indirect Objects

Preparation

1. Demonstrate the use of indirect objects before looking at the Spotlight Box. Use the classroom environment to create examples.

2. Hand a pencil to a student—"Paco," for example—as the entire class watches. Then say, "I gave a pencil to Paco." Add," I gave Paco a pencil."

3. Repeat this with other students. Give out papers, books, and other things and then state what you did. Use both forms. Say, "I gave some papers to Eva. I gave Eva some papers."

4. Then gesture for one student to give a pencil to another student. After the student does so, ask the class yes/no questions such as the following: "Did I give Eva the pencil?" (No) "Did Paco give Eva the pencil?" (Yes)

5. Tell Eva and Paco to repeat the action, but this time turn around so you can't see the action. Then turn back around to face the class, and ask students to tell you what happened.

6. Write their response on the board. Correct the form, if necessary. On the board add the other statements that were previously practiced orally.

7. Underline the indirect objects. Tell learners that the underlined words are indirect objects and that the students are going to read more about them in the next Spotlight Box.

Presentation

After students have read the examples in the Spotlight Box, have pairs generate sentences with the verbs listed under *to* and *for*. Before students begin model with a volunteer if necessary.

Answers to Exercise 1

1. for   2. for   3. to   4. for   5. for

Exercise 2

Preparation

Choose a pair of students to write the sentences they produced in the Spotlight presentation on the board. Use one sentence to model how to delete *to* or *for*. Emphasize the movement of the indirect object pronoun. Ask for volunteers to come to the board and rewrite the other sentences without *for* or *to*.

Answers to Exercise 2

Mei: I bought you some furniture.

Tom: You did?

Mei: I bought you a table and lamp. I also ordered you four chairs.

Tom: Where are the chairs?

Mei: They'll send you the chairs tomorrow.

Tom: Who is this big pillow for?

Mei: That's not for you. I got my sister that pillow.

Workbook

Workbook page 55 can be assigned after students have completed Student Book page 111.

Person to Person

Preparation

1. Have students work in pairs to think about the last time they bought furniture, either in the United States or in their native countries. Students should generate as much vocabulary as possible.

2. Have students read over the conversations individually, and point out new or difficult words. Define and give examples for *perfect* and *cute*.

Presentation

1. To check comprehension, ask questions, or have the students prepare and ask questions of the class. Here are some examples:

   - What does Mei want the clerk to do?
   - What does Mei give the clerk?
   - Who did Nicole buy the jacket and purse for?
   - Where does Judy want to go with Nicole?
   - What did Mei get at the second-hand store?

2. Have students work in pairs to complete conversation.

3. Ask pairs to present their conversations to the class.

Reading for Real

Preparation

Make a Venn diagram on the board with the following headings: *Office Desk, Computer Desk*. Divide the class in half. One group will brainstorm the similarities between the two desks, and the other will try to think of the differences. Leave the diagram on the board for students to use in Exercise 3.

Presentation

Have students read the ads individually and name any unfamiliar or difficult words.

Extension

Have students in small groups discuss the following questions: What do the ads say is more important, price or quality? Do you agree? Ask volunteers to share their opinions with the class.

Exercise 3

Presentation

Have the class look at question 4. Ask for a volunteer to explain the marks after the numbers. If students are unfamiliar with them, explain that they are a symbol meaning *inches*.

Answers to Exercise 3

1. b.   2. a   3. b   4. b   5. a

Activity Masters

Activity Master 10-1 can be assigned after students have completed Student Book page 113.

Page 114

Culture Corner

Preparation

Draw a coupon on the board or on a transparency. Elicit from students the definition of *coupon*. If students are unfamiliar with the term, provide a definition. With the class discuss the various elements in a coupon, including the product name, cents off, the expiration date, and the bar code.

Presentation

1. Have students read the selection silently while you read it aloud. Ask them to point out any new or difficult words. Discuss this vocabulary with the class. New words may include *discounts, office products,* and *percent off.*

2. To check comprehension, tell small groups of students to write answers to the following questions in their notebooks:

   - What are coupons?
   - Where do you find coupons?
   - Why should people be careful with coupons?

Extension

1. Bring four or five identical sets of coupons to class. Distribute one coupon to each member of a small group. Each person in the group should talk about the coupon.

2. Photocopy one list of questions about the coupons for each group. Include the following questions:

   - What's the product?
   - Who in the group buys this product?
   - How much can you save?
   - Are there special conditions on size, number or type of product?
   - Is there an expiration date? If there is, what is it?

3. Each member should take a turn at being secretary and write the answers about another person's coupon as other members listen and assist. The paper should then go to the next secretary, and another person should share information about a coupon.

4. Each group shares its results with the class.

Page 115

Scene 2

Preparation

Write on the board *comparison shopping*. Then review Reading for Real, page 113. Elicit or explain that looking at two products to decide which is the better value is *comparison shopping*. Tell learners that Scene 2 is about comparison shopping.

Presentation

Ask the following questions about Scene 2:

- What are Tom and Mei looking at?
- Do they want a big desk or a small desk?
- In the second picture, why does Tom like that desk?
- In the third picture what does Mei tell Tom that makes him decide not to buy the desk?

Extension

Have pairs of students role-play the Scene for the class in one of several ways. Bring in props or costumes to make the activity more interesting.

Option 1: Students can perform the lines as written. You can assign pairs or let students choose their own partners.

Option 2: Students can make a simple substitution in some lines (inserting something they would like to buy, for example).

Option 3: More advanced students can ad-lib a conversation on the topic treated in the Scene or imagine they are in a conversation with the characters in the Scene.

Sound Bites

Preparation

1. To prepare students to hear comparisons, ask students to compare two local restaurants. Ask questions such as the following:
   - Which restaurant is larger?
   - Which restaurant is less expensive?
   - Which one has better service?
   - Which one do you like better? Why?

2. Have students write the answers individually in their notebooks, then share them with the class.

Presentation

1. Point out to students that they will hear three conversations and that they will make three check marks, one for conversation 1, one for conversation 2, and one for conversation 3.

2. Play the tape of the conversations or read them to the class.

Listening Script

1. Mei: Look at this wood desk. It has space for your computer. And I like the color. It's beautiful!

   Tom: Hey, this metal one is better. It has more drawers. And it's less expensive too.

   Mei: It's less expensive? OK, let's buy it.

2. Woman 1:   I like this blue chair. You should buy it. It's comfortable. And hey, what a good price!

   Woman 2:   No, I think this black chair is better. It's larger. And look, the blue one has a small hole in the seat.

   Woman 1:   Oh, you're right. You should buy the black one.

3. Man 1:   I'll get this twelve-hundred dollar computer. It has everything I need. And the price is lower than the other computers.

   Man 2:   You're right. This computer costs fifteen hundred dollars. And it has less power than the twelve-hundred-dollar computer.

Answers to Sound Bites

1. the metal desk   2. the black chair   3. the twelve-hundred-dollar computer

Page 116

Spotlight on Comparative Adjectives

Preparation

Point to two items in the classroom and make comparisons using comparative adjectives. For example, point to a student's desk and to your desk and say, "My desk is bigger than your desk. Your desk is smaller then my desk." Tell students that more examples of comparative adjectives are in the next Spotlight Box.

Exercise 4

Presentation

Have students complete the dialogue individually. Ask pairs of students to perform it for the class. With the class discuss any answers students are unsure of.

Answers to Exercise 4

1. better   2. more comfortable   3. more expensive   4. smaller

Workbook

Workbook pages 56 and 57 can be assigned after students have completed Student Book page 116.

Spotlight on *Could*

Preparation

1. Generate some questions or statements about the class with the various uses of *could*. One way to do this is to put the word *could* on a transparency. Hold up the transparency and point to the overhead projector in a far corner of the room. Say, "Could someone help me move the projector? I can't move it by myself. Maybe two student volunteers could move the projector for me." After you get some student volunteers to move the projector, turn it on and put up the transparency with the word *could* on it.

2. Repeat the story and point to the word *could* when you use it. Tell students that more examples of how we use this word are in the next Spotlight Box.

Extension

Go over the preparation questions again. Analyze how *could* is used. Then choose the correct usage from the meanings listed in the Spotlight Box.

Exercise 5

Preparation

1. In small groups ask students to discuss the time when they were moving to the United States. Did they do everything themselves? What could they do? What couldn't they do? Why?

2. Tell students the story is about someone who is moving into a new apartment.

Answers to Exercise 5

Note: Answers to Exercise 6 are in parentheses here.

1. couldn't (A)   2. Could (B)   3. could (C)   4. couldn't (A)
5. Could (B)   6. could (C)   7. could (C)   8. could (C)

Exercise 6

Preparation

Write a list of sentences using the three meanings of *could* on the board. Tell students to work in pairs to copy them in their notebooks, and label them with the correct meaning: A (for ability in the past), B (for requests), or C (for future possibility). Review the correct answers with the class.

Answers to Exercise 6

See Exercise 5 above.

Workbook

Workbook page 58 can be assigned after students have completed Student Book page 117.

Activity Masters

Activity Master 10-2 can be assigned after students have completed Student Book page 117.

Get Graphic

Preparation

In small groups have students think of reasons why Tom would need a fax machine for his new shop.

Answers to Exercise 7

1. c   2. b   3. a

In Your Experience

Presentation

1. Photocopy a blank chart (and/or an overhead transparency of one) similar to the one in the book and distribute one copy per group.

2. Discuss with the class where in the newspaper to find the kinds of ads listed in the Get Graphic chart. For example, the yard sale ads would be in the classified ads section. The discount store and the office supply store may have ads on a separate sheet of paper in the middle of the newspaper. Some ads may be in magazines, on bulletin boards at the supermarket, or in posters at school.

3. Give each group one entire newspaper with ad inserts included, if possible. Have team members take apart the newspaper to investigate sections separately and report their findings to the group.

4. If fax machine ads are hard to find, substitute ads for TVs, telephones, or computers. Ideally, each team will work on a different item.

5. Each member fills out one ad on the chart, and a group reporter shares the chart and the findings with the class. (Using an overhead transparency of the chart may be the most time-efficient method for the presentations.)

Issues and Answers

Preparation

Show a credit card to the class. Ask students to tell you what it is and how to use it. Then show a credit card application form. Ask students to guess what information the credit card company wants.

Presentation

Have students read all the sentences in the chart. Discuss any words that are unfamiliar to the class. Ask the class which meaning of *could* is used. If students do not answer "future possibility," ask them to review the meanings presented on page 117.

Wrap-Up

Presentation

1. Define *average*.

2. To make the activity more challenging and interesting, have students give additional facts to consider. This could be group work, with each group member providing an additional fact to share on a slip of paper. Here are some examples:

   - In April, Tom would like to work in the evening. (He needs a lamp in April.)
   - His friend gave Tom a lot of books after doing some spring cleaning in May. (Tom needs a bookcase in May.)

Activity Masters

Activity Master 10-2 can be assigned after students have completed page 120.

Preparation

1. Have students form groups of four.

2. Have each student in the class write his or her name on a slip of paper.

3. Pass around a bag for students to put their slips in. Then, mix the slips inside the bag. Tell students they will be choosing a name to give a gift to from the bag.

4. Have each student draw a name from the bag. If the student draws his or her name or the name of someone from the same group, have him or her put the slip back and draw another name.

5. Distribute handouts and discuss the additional instructions, rules, and examples on the master before groups work independently. Stress to students that this activity is to practice the language of gift giving and that they don't actually have to give gifts to anyone. This is just for fun!

Presentation

1. Circulate to facilitate discussion and to monitor progress. If a group has no idea what one of its gift recipients would like, tell students to send someone (the group reporter) to interview the person and report back to the group. This provides excellent communication practice.

2. Encourage groups to be creative with their homemade gift ideas. Ask if anyone in the group is an artist, a baker, a musician, a seamstress, or a carpenter, for example. Have them brainstorm gift ideas based on their skills and talents. Remind them to include on the chart the estimated worth of each homemade gift.

Extension

A lesson on writing thank-you notes would be appropriate and fun.

Workbook

Workbook pages 59 and 60 can be assigned after students have completed Student Book page 120.

ANSWERS TO PROGRESS CHECKS

Progress Check A

Speak or Write

1. Mei is unhappy because she wants to buy a desk and chairs for her husband, but she only has $150.

2. Mei could find more bargains in a yard sale.

3. Answers will vary.

Listening Script

Answers are underlined.

Mei helped Tom with his new shop. First, (1) <u>Mei</u> bought a table and a lamp (2) <u>for</u> (3) <u>Tom</u>. Next, (4) <u>Mei</u> ordered a couch (5) <u>for</u> him. The store sent it (6) <u>to</u> them right away. (7) <u>Tom</u> was really pleased. He cooked (8) <u>Mei</u> a delicious meal. (9) <u>Tom</u> also gave flowers (10) <u>to</u> (11) <u>Mei</u>.

Progress Check B

Language Structures

1. more expensive (or nicer)
2. nicer (or more expensive)
3. cheaper (or smaller)
4. smaller (or cheaper)
5. Answers will vary; better

Content

1. Yard sales   2. coupons   3. no guarantee   4. more   5. is not   6. budget

ANSWERS TO ACTIVITY MASTERS

Activity Master 10-1

Ad A

Brand: General Electronic

Price: $197

Qualities: 25", color, remote control

Ad B

Brand: SOONI

Price: $217

Qualities: 13", VCR too

Answers will vary. Here are some possible answers.

We choose the TV from Ad A because it is cheaper.

We choose the TV from Ad B because it is nicer. It has a TV and a VCR.

Activity Master 10-2

Answers will vary.

REPRODUCIBLE MASTER
UNIT 10

WORKBOOK ANSWERS

Practice 1

1. for   2. for   3. to   4. for   5. to

Practice 2

1. She bought him a table and lamp.

2. She also ordered him a couch.

3. The store sent them the couch right away.

4. He cooked Mei a delicious dinner.

5. He also gave her flowers.

Practice 3

1. bigger   2. more expensive   3. better   4. closer

5. longer   6. faster

Practice 4

1. more modern   2. older   3. busier   4. cheaper

5. more expensive   6. closer   7. better

Practice 6

The budget time line should show the following:

$100 for a trip—August

$150 for fall clothes—September

$200 for a new TV—October

$150 for Christmas presents—November

REPRODUCIBLE MASTER
UNIT 10   PROGRESS CHECK A

SPEAK OR WRITE

Look at the pictures from Unit 10. Use the questions below to talk
or write about each picture.

Questions

1. Why is Mei unhappy in picture 1?

2. Where could Mei find some bargains?

3. Where is your favorite place to shop for bargains? Why?

LISTEN

While you listen, write *Mei, Tom, to,* and *for* in the blanks to make
the story correct.

Mei helped Tom with his new shop. First, (1) _____

bought a table and a lamp (2) _____

(3) _____. Next, (4) _____ ordered a

couch (5) _____ him. The store sent it

(6) _____ them right away. (7) _____

was really pleased. He cooked (8) _____ a delicious

meal. (9) _____ also gave flowers

(10) _____ (11) _____.

PROGRESS CHECK B

LANGUAGE STRUCTURES

Read the ads for notebook binders. Make comparisons. Use the words below to complete the sentences.

better   smaller   nicer   cheaper

more expensive   Savemore   Better Buys

Savemore Discount Store—	**Better Buys Discount Shop—**
Binders!	Notebooks on Sale
3-ringed notebooks with pockets!	$2.00 —Black —
Large size—Holds 11" x 14" paper	8½"x 11" — Save!
$4.79 each—Beautiful colors!	

1. The notebooks at Savemore are _____.

2. The notebooks at Savemore are also _____.

3. The notebooks at Better Buys are _____.

4. The notebooks at Better Buys are also _____.

5. I'd buy one at _____ because those binders are _____.

CONTENT

Underline the best word to complete each sentence.

1. (*Yard sales, Discount stores*) have lower prices.

2. Be careful with (*comparative shopping, coupons*). You may buy something you don't need.

3. Something for sale in a newspaper want ad has (*a guarantee, no guarantee*).

4. The best quality items probably cost (*more, less*).

5. The best value (*is, is not*) always the lowest price.

6. A (*budget, credit card*) is a plan for saving and spending money.

Name _____ Date _____

ACTIVITY MASTER 10-1

MORE READING FOR REAL WITH GRAPHIC SKILLS

Read the two advertisements for different TVs at a discount electronics store. Then complete the chart below with information about each of the TVs. With a partner or a small group, decide which TV to buy. Write your choice on the line at the bottom of the page. Be ready to explain your choice to the rest of the class.

Ad A   Ad B

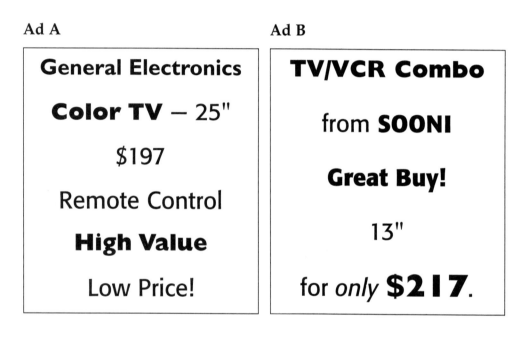

Brand	Price	Qualities

We choose the TV from Ad _____ because _____

_____

_____

_____

_____ .

GROUP PROBLEM SOLVING— FINDING THE PERFECT GIFT

Your teacher will ask each member of the group to pick a slip of paper out of a bag. Write the names of the students your group picked on the lines at the bottom of the page.

Choose a gift (or gifts) for each person that you picked. You can choose from the gifts below or think of your own homemade gifts. Your group cannot spend over $100, and you can't use the same gift twice. Talk about possible gifts and add some ideas to the homemade gifts list. Remember to use could, comparative adjectives, and indirect objects correctly. For example, say, "We could cook a meal for Bill. A meal is cheaper than a frying pan, and I know Bill likes good food!"

Write the gifts and the prices at the bottom of the page. Then read the names of the students and your group's gifts to the class. Explain why you gave the gifts you did.

Discount Store	Factory Outlet	Homemade Gifts	
TV $100	clock $30	a meal	$10
silver necklace $20	gold watch $35	_____	_____
frying pan $25	towels $15	_____	_____
cassette player $40	radio $15	_____	_____
silk flowers $10	tool box $25	_____	_____

1. name _____ gift _____ price _____

2. name _____ gift _____ price _____

3. name _____ gift _____ price _____

4. name _____ gift _____ price _____